JESUS'

Comforter is

MUHAMMAD

The Last and the Final Prophet of God

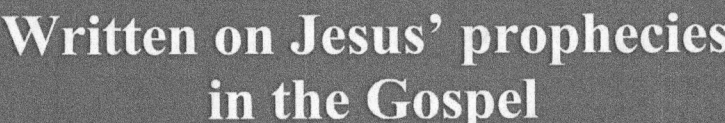

Written on Jesus' prophecies
in the Gospel

Dil R. Banu

WORKBOOK PRESS LLC
187 E Warm Springs Rd,
Suite B285 Las Vegas NV 89119 USA

Website: https://workbookpress.com/
Hotline: 1-888-818-4856
Email: admin@workbookpress.com

Ordering Information:

Quantity sales. Special discounts are available on quantity purchases by corporations, associations, and others. For details, contact the publisher at the address above.

Library of Congress Control Number:

ISBN-13:   978-1-965732-63-2 Paperback Version

REV. DATE: 08/30/2025

JESUS'

Comforter is

MUHAMMAD

The Last And The Final Prophet Of God

[Written on Jesus' prophecies in the Gospel]

Dil R. Banu

DEDICATION

Dedicated to all my Christian Missionary friends for their
valuable time and talk to help me write this book

CONTENTS

ACKNOWLEDGEMENTS

I'd first thank God-my Creator-Lord most humbly, gratefully, and endlessly to choose me for this noble job of writing and to help me complete it under His constant care and guidance. I also beg Him to kindly forgive me for all my negligence and mistakes that I might have shown or done due to my own ignorance and shortcomings.

I also ask God fervently to shower His endless mercy, love, and blessing for all the authors alive or dead, who helped me to write this book with valuable information and material which they obtained through their ceaseless effort, study, and research. I have added a list of their books in a bibliography at the end of this book.

I thank Anna, my precious and a devout Christian friend from the bottom of my heart. It is her question "Was Muhammad A Prophet?" which made me study, explore, and finally write this book. May God always bless her and her family with His endless love, mercy, and guidance!

I also thank Mr. Aaron Washington most gratefully for his review about my previous book ANNA ASKED WAS MUHAMMAD A PROPHET? [Her question is answered from the Bible and other major scriptures of the world]. It has certainly enhanced the weight and the worth of my book. I've added his review in the last part of this book.

I also like to express my thankful gratitude to all my learned friends for their valuable time to read the manuscript of this book and for their feedback which I found very inspiring.

Last but not the least, I would like to appreciate my wonderful daughter Tasmeea and son Shihab along with their most adorable spouses and children for their constant help, care, and support to continue with my study and writing undisturbed at this old age of my life.

I also want to convey my special and heart-felt thanks, gratitude, and appreciation to Abid Noor-my twenty years old beloved grandson for his spontaneous help and support in presenting the manuscript of my book to the publishers. May God kindly help him to stick to His Path and to strive for His Cause until the last moment of his life.

This book contains a part of my book "Anna Asked Was Muhammad A Prophet?" where I tried to describe Muhammad' advent mainly on Jesus' prophecies in the Gospel whom he called Comforter or Advocate.

Salutation to Prophet Muhammad and to all the messengers of God who were sent before him

I'd like to remind all my Muslim friends to ask God to bestow His endless mercy and blessing upon Prophet Muhammad and to all His messengers who were sent before him when they come across with their blessed names.

WHY I WROTE THIS BOOK?

I am a non-Arab Muslim by birth and practice. I am a retired lecturer from one of the prestigious colleges of my homeland Bangladesh. I settled in America more than three decades ago when I worked as a substitute teacher for a year. Then, I started running a family daycare in my rented apartment where most of my neighbors were Christians. During this period, I met many Christian missionaries who used to visit me often at my residence. The main purpose of their visit was to tell me about Jesus and what I needed to do to redeem my sins and to have eternal life in heaven. But I didn't find any such thing in the Gospel when I read it. Rather, I found the basic requirements for our way to heaven were the same as God has revealed in the Quran through His last Prophet Muhammad.

While talking to them about it, I felt astonished to know that most of them were not aware of Islam which God had established through Prophet Muhammad more than fourteen hundred years ago. So, the name of Muhammad as the last Prophet of God and the name of the Quran as His last or the final guidebook for all of mankind, also remained unknown to most of them. Or, if they knew anything at all, it was either wrong or misleading. For example, many of them mistook Muhammad-the Prophet of Islam in the seventh century Arabian desert for Elijah Muhammad, a black American and the founder of Nation of Islam in Chicago only a few decades ago.

Not only the Christian missionaries but many well-reputed evangelists and the elite among the Christians also have lots of reservations to accept Muhammad as a true Prophet of God. Some of them declared openly that he was an imposter. Some said he invented his religion Islam to serve his own purpose, while others said he wrote the Quran himself copying from here and there from the Old Testament and then claimed he received it from God. Some said Muhammad was the anti-Christ, and his only motive was to deviate the Christians from the teaching of Jesus.

It is mainly for them, I wrote this part separately from my book ANNA ASKED WAS MUHAMMAD A PROPHET? where I tried to narrate Muhammad's advent mainly on the prophecies of Jesus whom he called Comforter, Counselor or Advocate. All three names apply to Muhammad perfectly, but I chose the name Comforter from the Bible in King James'

Version. I believe, the devoted followers of Jesus Christ may take the message of my book seriously if I present to them with evidence from the Gospel that Muhammad was Jesus' Comforter whom he meant to come after him to testify of him (John 15:26), to remind the people of what he taught them (John 14:26), and to guide them all to the truth that God revealed through him and all his predecessors before him. (John 16:13)

With my warm regards to all my readers.

DIL R BANU
Maryland,
November 7, 2024

REFERENCE AND RESOURCES

Last of all, I like to inform my readers that the primary sources of my knowledge, information and reference to write this book are the two Holy Scriptures-the Bible and the Quran. For the Bible, I consulted the King James Version [KJV], New International Version [NIV] and Revised Standard Version [RSV]. But I quoted all the prophecies on Muhammad's advent and other issues related to the topic either from KJV or NIV.

For the Quran, I consulted the meaning and interpretation of the renowned scholars like Ibn-Kathir, Mufti Muhammad Shafi, A.Yusuf Ali, Muhammad M. Pickthal and Muhammad Farooq-i-Azam Malik, but I quoted the meaning of the verses mostly from the last three of them. And sometimes I changed a bit in their words while keeping their meaning unchanged. I did so to make it sound easy and simple for the common and ordinary people of the Western world. I have also added a bibliography of the books that I used for study, information and reference at the end of this book.

WHAT IS A PROPHECY?

Before we enter into the main topic of our discussion, I should mention first what do we mean by a prophecy? A prophecy usually refers to a speech or a statement about some future events or occurrences made in advance by a Prophet or a Chosen person of God. They usually make those prophecies being inspired by God. It contains some distinctive words or phrases which help the people to know and verify the truth when they occur or manifest according to the Pre-set timetable of God.

The Bible also tells us in Deut 18:21-22 to use the prophecy as a sign or a criterion to identify a true Prophet of God from a false claimant. The reason for that is obvious and understood. God chose this unique criterion to identify His true prophets from the false claimants because there is none but His true prophets who could make accurate prophecies being inspired by His infinite knowledge and wisdom. But the false prophets usually make their prophecies based on their own imagination, insight, or their acquired knowledge, which may sometimes be partially true. In that case, we should only accept them as the true prophets of God whose prophecies became fulfilled as they said. According to that criterion, Muhammad should be accepted as a true Prophet of God, because most of his prophecies that he made more than fourteen hundred years ago, became true by this time and many of them are still occurring in and around us. I've narrated some of them while explaining Jesus' prophecies about his Comforter/Advocate where he said: *And he will show you things to come*. (John 16:13)

In this context, we also need to remember that prophecies made by a true Prophet of God may not always come true. It happened so to Jonah who left Nineveh warning his people of a terrible disaster in three days to destroy them all for their sinful life and disobedience to God. But both the Bible and the Quran tell us it did not occur because the entire people of Nineveh gave up their wrong-doings and returned to God through sincere repentance, remorse, and rectifying their ways of life, soon Jonah left the city being disappointed with them.

The Bible also contains a series of prophecies about the arrival of some distinguished prophets like Moses, Isaac, Elias, Jesus, and other chosen persons of God. Similarly, both parts of the Bible also contain numerous prophecies about the arrival of Muhammad-the last and the final Prophet of God. But people hardly knew about it because most of those prophecies have remained unnoticed, uninformed, or unexplored. Besides that, many of those prophecies were mistaken for Jesus when they were meant exclusively for the Arab Prophet Muhammad. Jesus' prophecies in the Gospel about his Comforter or Advocate were also mistaken for the Holy Ghost or the Holy Spirit.

Similarly, Muhammad's advent in other major scriptures of the world also remained unknown to most of the people because those prophecies were made in different languages, and they were also composed in allegories, metaphors or unintelligible riddles which was too difficult to comprehend even by their own scholars and learned people.

My heart-felt thanks and gratitude go to those truth-seeking, dedicating, and persevering scholars of both Eastern and the Western world, who finally overcame those difficulties and brought the hidden meaning of those prophecies to the knowledge and understanding of the common people like me and others. In this book, I only tried to explain those prophecies of Jesus where he mentioned some characteristics about his Comforter or Advocate which pinpoint to none but the Arab Prophet Muhammad who arrived after him as the last and the final Prophet of God along with His last guidebook-the Quran.

You may say to yourselves, "How can we know when a message has not been spoken by the LORD?

If what a prophet proclaims in the name of the LORD does not take place or come true, that is a message the LORD has not spoken. That prophet has spoken presumptuously, so do not be alarmed (Deut. 21-22)

CHAPTER ONE

Jesus' Comforter is Muhammad-the Last and the Final Prophet of God

When the Comforter comes, whom I will send to you from the Father-the Spirit of truth who goes out from the Father-he will testify about me. (John 15:26)

My Christian friends may feel surprised to know that Jesus has made a series of prophecies about Muhammad's arrival after him as the last and the final Prophet of God. I chose to begin with the prophecy in John 15:26 where he said:

When the Comforter comes, whom I will send to you from the Father-the Spirit of truth who goes out from the Father-he will testify about me.

Before I explain this prophecy, I need to inform both my Christian and non-Christian readers that the Bible in the King James Version mentioned Muhammad as Comforter, while RSV mentioned him as Counselor, and NIV mentioned him as Advocate. Though all three names match perfectly well with the meaning and implication of "Muhammad," I have chosen Comforter for my book. We shall check first how those names apply to the Arab Prophet Muhammad.

The history of religion tells us Jesus used to teach people in his native language Aramaic, which was translated first into Hebrew, from Hebrew to Greek, from Greek to English, and then to many other languages of the world. In that case, if we claim Jesus meant Muhammad to be his Comforter, Counselor or Advocate, we need to know first what he called Muhammad in Aramaic. I think my readers will understand my point better, if I first explain to them the meaning and implication of Muhammad-the name of the last Prophet of God. His other popular name is Ahmad.

According to the expert linguists in Arabic, Hebrew, and Aramaic the name "Muhammad" has been originated from the same root, which is *hmd* in Arabic, *hamdduit in* Hebrew, *and himdath* in Aramaic, the meaning of which is praised one, praiseworthy, the most laudable, desire, desirable, glorified or altogether lovely. Though, "altogether lovely" has now been substituted

9

by "altogether desirable" in many modern versions of the Bibles, including the RSV. Interestingly, this substitution has been made while translating a prophecy of the Hebrew king and Prophet Solomon around 1600 BCE, where he mentioned Muhammad by name and adored him as his beloved and friend. He said:

> His mouth is most sweet: yea, he is altogether lovely.
> This is my beloved, and this is my friend. (sol. 5:16)

altogether lovely in the above-quoted statement has been translated from the Hebrew word *Mahammudim*. Except for the additional *im* at the end of the name, there is hardly any difference in the pronunciation of both Muhammad and Mahammud. The *im* at the end of Mahammud also needs a bit of clarification. In the language of Hebrew, an *im* at the end of a name indicates a royal plural to show respect or honor as it is done with the name *Elohim*, which is the plural form of *Eloha* but means the same One God in the Hebrew Bible. Solomon said *Mahammudim* instead of *Mahammud* to show his utmost respect for his beloved friend who arrived long after him as the last and the final Messenger of God.

In this context, I also like to inform my readers that Haggai-another Hebrew Prophet in the Old Testament of the Bible, has mentioned Muhammad as *the desire* of all nations who will arrive near the Sacred House of God at Makkah where the world-shaking religion Islam will be given to him. (Hag 2:7&9)

At this point, any of my inquisitive readers may want to know how those translated names of Muhammad be substituted for *advocate* or *Comforter!* I shall now come to that.

While translating the Bible from Hebrew or Aramaic to Greek, the translators used two names for Muhammad. One of them is *periclytos* and the other one is *paracletos.* The meaning of *periclytos* corresponds directly to the meaning of *hmd, hamdduit,* or *himdath* that I mentioned before. But for some unknown reason, the translators of the Bible from Greek to English chose the word *paracletos* the meaning of which is comforter, advocate, counselor, kind, friendly, or 'one being sought for help.'

Whatever their reason was, we may ignore it because the meaning of *paracletos* also describes Muhammad perfectly well. All his pagan kith and kin of Makkah also knew him as a kind, comforting, and a friendly person whom they constantly sought for help, advice, or counsel long before he claimed himself a Prophet of God. Since no prophet arrived yet by this name after Jesus left, we can assume rightly that he meant none but Muhammad when he called him Comforter, Counselor or Advocate.

We may now check why Jesus mentioned his Comforter as *the spirit of truth* and how it matches perfectly with the conduct or character of Prophet Muhammad who arrived nearly six hundred years after his ascent to heaven.

"The Spirit of Truth" in John 15:26, describes Muhammad perfectly

The Spirit of Truth usually refers to a person who remains true to his words, deeds and thoughts under all circumstances of his life. Jesus being an inspired messenger of God mentioned Muhammad rightly *as the spirit of truth*. We can verify the truth in Muhammad's biographies written by the open-minded scholars-both Muslims and non-Muslims. At this point, it is also important to note that most of the pagan Arabs rejected him with the accusation of being a sorcerer, possessed, poet or highly ambitious when he declared himself a Prophet of God at his age forty, but they accused him less of being a liar, cheat or a hypocrite.

It is also a recorded part in the history of Islam that when Heraclius-the Byzantine Emperor, received a letter from Prophet Muhammad inviting him and his people to Islam, he called the pagan Arab traders who were then visiting his country. The emperor asked Abu Sufyan-their leader, "Did you ever find Muhammad telling a lie before his claim to Prophethood?"

He replied that he had not. Then Heraclius questioned him about the Prophet's conduct and manners with his people. Abu Sufyan replied, "Muhammad is born and brought up in a noble family. He is honest and truthful, and he has never broken a pledge...."

Besides that, we also came to know that the pagans of Makkah trusted none but Muhammad to keep their valuables when they used to leave Makkah for travel or business. At the time of the Prophet's migration to Medina to save his life from the persecutors of Makkah, he did not forget about their valuables which he had with him at that time. The Prophet asked his cousin Ali to return the deposited items under his pledge to the right persons after he leaves. We can take it as an unprecedented example of his integrity, honesty, and love for truth which he showed to keep his pledge with the infidels at that crucial moment of his life. I think no more example is required to believe that Jesus was right when he mentioned his Comforter as *the Spirit of truth*. We shall now check why Jesus needed a truthful man from God to testify of him after he leaves?

Why did Jesus say when the Comforter would come after him, he would testify of him?

Frankly speaking, when I read this part for the first time, I wondered why Jesus-a noble and a beloved Prophet of God needed a truthful person to testify of him after he leaves? I was surprised because I knew a man usually needed a reliable witness to testify of his innocence, if he was accused by someone with some false charges which he didn't commit. In that case, who could frame Jesus-a mighty Prophet of God with some false accusations that he would need some reliable testifier to make him free from that?

I'm not sure whether this type of question has ever bothered any devoted followers of Jesus. But I think it has certainly bothered Jesus a lot because being an inspired Messenger of God he was aware of the day when the false prophets would appear with their false doctrines in his name and deviate his followers from the eternal truth of the First Commandment that he preached and practiced himself all through his life. Though Jesus knew it was inevitable, he left for his people some precautionary notes about the arrival of some false prophets who would deviate them with their false doctrines from what he taught them by the command of God.

Jesus' warning about the arrival of the false prophets.

(Matt. 7:15) Beware of the false prophets, which come to you in sheep's clothing, but inwardly they are ravening wolves.

(Matt. 24:4–5) Take heed that no man deceives you. For many shall come in my name, saying, I am Christ; and shall deceive many.

(Matt. 15:9) But in vain they do worship me, teaching for doctrines the commandments of men.

(Matt. 7:21) Not everyone who says to me, Lord, Lord, will enter the kingdom of heaven, but only the one who does the will of my Father who is in heaven.

(Matt. 15:13-14) He [Jesus] replied, every plant that my heavenly Father has not planted will be pulled up by the roots. Leave them; they are blind guides. If the blind lead the blind, both will fall into a pit.

Jesus took their deviation seriously because he also knew that his people would believe and practice those man-made laws in his name after he leaves when he would have no control over them. It is the only reason Jesus needed a testifier from God who would tell the world openly who he really was, why he was sent for, what he taught his people in the name of God, what he never taught them and what they began practicing in his name after he left. With the answer to all those questions and the final commands of God, Muhammad was sent along with His last guidebook- the Quran for all of mankind.

We may now check in the Quran what are those issues that most of the devoted Christians believe and practice in the name of Jesus which he never taught them and how God made him free from that through his Comforter meaning Muhammad who was sent after him.

God testifies through Muhammad about Jesus' virgin birth as a sign of His absolute power and authority

From the contents of the following statements of the Quran, we have learned about Jesus' virgin birth as a sign of God's absolute power and authority over everything in the entire heavens and earth.

: And mention the one who guarded her chastity [Jesus' virgin mother Mary]. I blew into her My command and made her and her son a sign for the world. (21:91)

: When the angels said, "O Mary! Verily, God gives you the glad tidings of a Word [Be], from Him, his name will be Christ Jesus..." (3:45)

: She said, "My Lord, how will I have a son when no man has touched me?" The Angel said, "Such is God; He creates what He wills. When He decrees a matter, He only says to it 'Be' and it is. (3:47)

: Indeed, the example of Jesus to God is like that of Adam. He created him from dust; then He said to him, "Be," and he was. (3:59)

Based on those Quranic statements, we believe Jesus' virgin birth took place by God's commanding word "Be" as a sign or manifestation of His absolute power, authority and knowledge over everything in the entire heavens and earth. The Book of Genesis also tells us when God wanted to create light and other things in the heavens and earth, He just said to it "Let there be" and it was.

As Mary conceived Jesus when God said "Be," we also regard him as the "Word" of God. But like the devoted followers of Jesus, we don't find any mystery or mysticism in his being called the "Word" of God. I've said so because following the statement in John 1:1, most of the Christians claim the "Word" was with God from the beginning and the "Word" was God. Not only that, from the statement in John 1:14, they also claim the "Word" referring to God was made flesh in the form of His only *begotten* Jesus and then appeared to dwell among them full of grace and truth.

In other words, they believe God was born through Virgin Mary in the form of His only *begotten* Jesus and lived with them gracefully for a short period of his life. With this thought in mind, most of the Christians believe Jesus was a deity and worship him as God Incarnate. In this context, it is also important to note that nowhere in the Gospel Jesus has ever told his people or given any indication that he was God in the human-form, and they should worship him as God or along with God as one and the same. Rather, Like all his predecessors, Jesus has told them all clearly that God is their only LORD, and no one deserves their worship except Him. I have quoted below a few of those verses from both parts of the Bible to justify my claim.

: Hear, O Israel: The LORD our God is one LORD. And thou shalt love the LORD thy God with all thine heart, and with all thy soul, and with all thy might. (Duet 6:4–5)

: You alone are the LORD, you made the heavens, even the highest heavens, and all their starry hosts, the earth and all that is on it, the seas and all that is in them. You give life to everything, and the multitudes of heaven worship you. (Nehemiah 9:6)

: Remember the former things of old: for I am God, and there is none else; I am God, and there is none like me. (Isa. 46:9)

…HEAR, O' ISRAEL; THE LORD OUR GOD IS ONE LORD: AND THOU SHALT LOVE THE LORD, THY GOD WITH ALL THY HEART, AND WITH ALL THY SOUL, AND WITH ALL THY MIND AND WITH ALL THY STRENGTH: this is the first commandment. (Mark 12:29–30)

Jesus said to Mary Magdalene, "Touch me not; for I am not yet ascended to my Father: but go to my brethren and say unto them, I ascend unto my Father, and your Father, and to my God, and to your God." (John 20:17)

God testifies through Muhammad about Jesus' being His only begotten as a monstrous lie

The Quran tells us that the Christians' claim on Jesus' being His only begotten son as a monstrous lie.

: They (Christians) say: 'God has begotten a son!' Glory be to Him! He is self-sufficient! Everything in the heavens and earth belongs to Him. Have you any proof for what you say? Would you ascribe to Him something about which you have no knowledge? (10:68)

: It is not [befitting] for Allah to take a son; exalted is He! When He decrees an affair, He only says to it, "Be," and it is. (19:35)

: And they [the Christians] say: The Most Gracious [God] has begotten a son! Indeed, they have told a most monstrous lie! For which the skies are ready to burst, the earth is to split asunder, and the mountains are to fall in utter ruin, that they ascribe a son to the most Gracious [God]. For it is not befitting to the Compassionate God that He should beget a son. (19:88–92)

[To Muhammad] Say: He is God, The One and Only. The Eternal, The Absolute; He begets not, nor is He begotten; and there is none comparable to Him. (112:1–4)

In this context, I like to remind my Christian friends that in some places of the Gospel Jesus called God as his Father in heaven and him as His son. We believe Jesus said so out of his deep love for God and to feel himself closer to God. But by this call, Jesus never meant he was truly begotten by God and therefore both are equal or have the same status as his followers claim. They probably have remained oblivious to those statements in the Gospel where Jesus made it clear to all that the status of God is the highest of all and he is but one of His servants. Jesus has also mentioned that he never said or did anything but by the command of God. Truth can be checked in the following statements of the Gospel.

….If ye loved me, ye would rejoice, because I said, I go unto the Father: For my Father is greater than I. (John 14:28)

: Very truly I tell you, no servant is greater than his master, nor is a messenger greater than the one who sent him. (John 13:16)

Then Jesus said unto them, "when ye have lifted up the son of man, then shall ye know that I am he, and that I do nothing of myself; but as my father hath taught me, I speak of these things. (John 8:28)

: For, I have not spoken of myself; but the Father which sent me, he gave me a commandment, what I should say, and what I should speak.

: And I know that his commandment is life everlasting: whatsoever I speak therefore, even as the Father said unto me, so I speak. (John 12:49–50)

In the quoted verses Jesus has made it clear to all that the status of God is the highest of all and he was sent by Him as His messenger only to please Him through keeping His commands. Let me provide more evidence from the Bible and the history of Jewish Tradition and culture for my readers to understand the true meaning or implication of the "son of God" and the "son of man."

"Son of God" refers to a loyal, righteous and God-fearing person

From the narration of the Jewish Tradition and culture, we also came to know that the Jews used to call a loyal, righteous, and a God-fearing person as the "Son of God." I've quoted below a few of those verses from both parts of the Bible to justify my point.

: I [David] will declare the decree: the LORD hath said unto me, thou art my son; this day have I begotten thee. (Psalm 2:7)

[To Moses] And thou shalt say unto Pharaoh, thus saith the LORD, Israel is my son, even my firstborn. (Exodus 4:22)

: When the morning stars sang together, and all the sons of God shouted for joy. (Job 38:7)

: And lo a voice from heaven, saying, this is my beloved Son, in whom I am well pleased. (Matt. 3:17)

In the quoted verses, we don't find any difference in the status, place, or position among the sons of God. Rather, we find all the noble, righteous, obedient, and the beloved servants or the messengers of God were addressed as the "sons of God."

I also have quoted below two statements from the Gospel of Mark and Luke, concerning a remark made by a centurion about Jesus, after he saw him die on the cross.

: And when the centurion, who stood there in front of Jesus, saw how he died, he said, "Surely this man was the Son of God!" (Mark 15:39)

: The centurion, seeing what had happened, praised God and said, "Surely this was a righteous man." (Luke 23:47)

In the Gospel of Luke, the term "Son of God" was replaced by a "Righteous man," because people of Jesus' time as I mentioned before, used to address a noble and righteous man as the "Son of God".

"Son of man" refers to a human being

The scholars in the Jewish language and culture tell us, people of Jesus' time used to call a human being as "son of man." According to the practice of that time, Jesus who was born and brought up in a Jewish family also called himself "son of man," though he had no human father. By the "son of man"

Jesus simply meant he was a human being or a man of flesh and blood.

In this context, I also like to remind my readers that Jesus called himself the "Son of man" eighty-one times [Math 30 times; Mark 14 times; Luke 25 times; John 12 times.], whereas he referred himself as the "Son of God" only six times [John 3:16-18; 5:25; 10:36; 11:4].

It is for the information of my readers, I also like to point out that some amendments have been made in the following verses regarding the status of the "Son of God."

For example, in the narration of the New World Translation of the Holy Scriptures, the term "Son of God" has been eliminated from the Gospel of Mark 1.1. The NIV says in a footnote that some manuscripts do not have the Son of God.

Another important elimination regarding "Son of God" was made in Acts 8:37 in the Version of King James where Philip said to the eunuch:

"If thou believest with all thine heart, thou mayest. And he answered and said, "I believe that Christ is the Son of God."

But the entire verse has now been eliminated from the New International Version of the Bible, with a brief footnote at the bottom 'it was found in some manuscripts.'

The situation got more complex, when the word "begotten" was added to the term "Son of God" to make Jesus' status equal to God.

"Begotten" has been removed from the Gospel of John

Most of my missionary friends used to quote the following statement in support of their eternal life through having faith in Jesus' sacrifice for their sin.

:For God so loved the world, that He gave His only Begotten Son, that whosoever believeth in him should not perish, but have everlasting life. (John 3:16)

But the keyword "Begotten" in John 3:16, has now been removed from all the modern Versions of the Bible. They found the word "Begotten" came from the Greek word monogenes, which means unique or special. It describes Jesus accurately. We also believe he is unique and special for his miraculous birth, the miracles he performed, his crucifixion, his reappearance to his disciples three days after his burial, and above all, his ascent to Heaven alive. All these extraordinary episodes of his life have truly made him a unique and a specia Messenger of God not only in the history of religion, but also in the history of mankind.

God testifies through Muhammad that Jesus was sent from the House of Israel for the guidance of his own people

There are many statements in the Quran which tell us Jesus was sent from the House of Israel for the guidance of his own people-the misguided Jews. I have quoted below some of them to justify my point.

: Behold! The angels said, "O Mary! Allah has chosen you and purified you, above the women of all nations. ... Allah will teach your son the Book, the Wisdom, the Torah, and the Gospel, and will make him a Messenger to the children of Israel. (3:42)

: The Messiah, son of Mary, was not but a Messenger; [other] messengers have passed away before him. And his mother was a chaste and a truthful woman. (5:75)

: Then the people asked her [Mary]: "How can we talk to one who is a child in the cradle? He [Jesus] said, I am indeed a servant of God; He has given me revelation and made me a Prophet. (19:29)

The Gospel also tells us Jesus was sent from the House of Israel for the guidance of his own people

The people of Jesus' time also knew he was sent from the House of Israel for the guidance of his own people-the misguided Jews. Truth can be checked in the following statements of the Gospel.

: But he [Jesus] answered and said, I am not sent but unto the lost sheep of the house of Israel. (Matt. 15:24)

: And the multitude said, this is Jesus the prophet of Nazareth of Galilee. (Matt. 21:11)

: "What things?" he asked. "About Jesus of Nazareth," they replied. "He was a prophet, powerful in word and deed before God and all the people. ....(Luke 24:19)

After the people saw the sign Jesus performed, they began to say, "Surely this is the Prophet who is to come into the world." (John 6:14)

: Now this is eternal life: that they know you; the only true God, and Jesus Christ, whom you have sent. (John 17:3)

God testifies through Muhammad that Jesus was also sent to Call his people to worship of none but One God as did all his predecessors before him

The Quran also tells us that Jesus was also sent to call his people to worship none but One God as did all his predecessors before him. Out of countless verses in the Quran, I have quoted below only a few of them.

Noah said, "O my people, worship Allah! You have no other God but Him. I fear for you the punishment of a dreadful day!" (7:59)

: To the people of A'd, I sent their brother Hud. He said: "O my people! Worship Allah, you have no other God but Him. You are not but the inventors of falsehood." (11:50)

: To the people of Madyan I sent their brother Shuaib who said, "O my people! Worship Allah, and look forward to the Last Day, and do not transgress in the land wickedly." (29:36)

Abraham who was born and brought up in a pagan family and a community, did not belong to them. He rejected their idol-worship from his early age and became a staunch believer and a worshiper of One Almighty God as the Creator and the Controller of everything in the entire heavens and earth. Being inspired by that knowledge Abraham declared, "Verily, I have turned my face being upright to Him Who has created the heavens and earth, and I do not belong to the idolators." (6:79)

[God says to Moses] "I have chosen you. So, listen to what I reveal to you. Verily, I am Allah. There is no God but Me. So, worship Me alone and establish regular prayer for my remembrance." (20:13-14)

I [Jesus] am appointed to confirm that which is before me from the Torah and to make lawful to you some of that which was forbidden to you. Now I have come to you with a sign from your Lord. So fear God and obey me.

: And when Jesus brought clear proofs, he said, "I have come to you with wisdom and to make clear to you some of that over which you differ, so fear Allah and obey me. Indeed, Allah is my Lord and your Lord, so worship Him. This is a straight path. (43:63-64)

When Muhammad was sent after Jesus, he was also commanded to proclaim the worship of none but One God among his people as did all his predecessors before him. Let me quote some statements from the Quran in support of that.

: Say [O Muhammad!] we believe in God and in what has been revealed to us, and what was sent down to Abraham, Ishmael, Isaac, Jacob, and their descendants; and what was given to Moses, Jesus, and other prophets from their Lord; We make no distinction between one another among them, and we submit to God as Muslim (3:84).

: Say [O Muhammad!] "As for me, surely my Lord has guided me to a straight path, Right Religion, the faith of Abraham-the monotheist and he was not of them who worshiped God in association with others. (6:161)

[To Muhammad] Tell them, "I am but a human being like you; the revelation is sent to me to declare that your God is One God; therefore, whoever hopes to meet with his Lord, let him do good deeds and join no partner in the worship of his Lord. (18:110)

In this context, I would like to remind my Christian friends that both parts of the Bible also tell us that all the prophets of God including Jesus are also known to ask their people to believe in One God and to worship none but Him as their Creator-Lord and as their only true Guide and Savior. Truth can be checked in the following verses of the Bible.

Evidence from the Old Testament of the Bible

[God says to Abraham] And I will establish my covenant between me and thee and thy seed after thee in their generations for an everlasting covenant, to be a God unto thee, and to thy seed after thee. (Gen. 17:7)

And God spoke unto Moses, and said unto him, "I am the LORD: And I appeared unto Abraham, unto Isaac, and unto Jacob, by the name of God Almighty, but by my name Jehovah was I not known to them." (Exo. 6:2–3)

[Being commanded by God Moses said to his people], "Hear, O Israel: The LORD our God is one LORD. And thou shalt love the LORD thy God with all thine heart, and with all thy soul, and with all thy might." (Duet 6:4–5)

"Fear the LORD your God, serve him only and take your oaths in his name. Do not follow other gods of the people around you. (Duet 6:13-14)

[God declares through Prophet Isaiah], I, even I, am the LORD; and beside me there is no savior. (Isa. 43:11)

: Remember the former things of old: for I am God, and there is none else; I am God, and there is none like me. (Isa. 46:9)

[God says through Prophet Jeremiah], And, go not after other gods to serve them, and to worship them, and provoke me not to anger with the works of your hands; and I will do you no hurt. (Jer. 25:6)

Evidence from the Gospel of Jesus

Jesus, the last Prophet of God from the House of Israel also conveyed the same message to his people about God's being One and to worship none but Him.

When one of the teachers of the law asked him, "Of all the Commandments, which is the most important?"

"The most important one," answered Jesus, "is this: Hear, O Israel: The Lord our God, the Lord is one. Love the Lord your God with all your heart and with all your soul and with all your mind and with all your strength. (Mark 12:28-30)

In reply to all the lucrative offers of Satan (Matt. 4:8-9), Jesus said to him, "Away from me, Satan! For it is written, ' Worship the Lord your God, and serve him only. (Matt. 4:10)

God testifies through Muhammad that Jesus never taught his people to worship him as God or as one of the Gods in the Trinity

In the following verses of the Quran, God has testified through Muhammad that Jesus never taught his people to worship him as God or as one of the Gods in the Trinity.

: "O people of the Book! [Meaning the Christians] Do not transgress on the limits of your religion. Speak nothing but the truth about God. The Messiah Jesus, the son of Mary was but a Messenger of God and His word "Be" which He bestowed upon Mary and a Spirit from Him. So, believe in God and His messengers and do not say "Trinity;" desist-it is better for you. God is only One Deity. Exalted is He above having a son. To Him belongs whatever is in the heavens and whatever is on the earth. And sufficient is God as the Disposer of all affairs. (4:171)

: Certainly, they have disbelieved who say: "God is Christ-the son of Mary" while the Christ has said, "O children of Israel! Worship God; my Lord and your Lord." Whoever worships God in association with others, God has forbidden him paradise, and his refuge is the fire of hell." ..... (5:72)

Interestingly, the Gospel of Jesus doesn't contain a single verse where the Christians are commanded to worship One God in the union of three. Naturally, because the doctrine of the Trinity is a man-made product from the Council of Nicaea, and it became a mandetory part of Christian Faith about

325 years after Jesus' ascent to heaven. In other words, what the scholars of the Bible have recently discovered, the Quran has mentioned it more than fourteen hundred years ago through Jesus' testifier Muhammad.

God testifies through Muhammad that Jesus did not die on the Cross for the sin of mankind

The Quran tells us Jesus did not die on the Cross for the sin of mankind as his followers claim about him. In the following verse of the Quran we are told:

[And they- the Jews were cursed] for their disbelief and uttering terrible slanders against Mary.

And for their saying [in boast], 'We have killed the Messiah Jesus, son of Mary, the Messenger of God.' But they did not kill him. Nor they crucified him but so it was made appear to them. And those who differ are full of doubts with no certain knowledge about it. They only follow a mere conjecture; they certainly killed him not.

Rather, God raised him up to Himself. And God is Ever Mighty, All Wise. (4:156-158)

Interestingly, many people of Jesus' time also believed he was not crucified. Some used to believe that it was Judas-one of the disciples of Jesus who took thirty pieces of silver from the pro-Roman Jewish elders to make his Master known to the Roman soldiers, was transformed into Jesus after he completed his job; and it was him who was arrested and crucified in his place as a punishment from God. Jesus' mother and his other disciples knew about it when Jesus appeared to them and told them what happened.

Some said one of Jesus' followers who resembled him, was arrested and crucified. Some said a devoted follower of Jesus agreed willingly to be transformed like him and be arrested and crucified in his place, when Jesus asked his disciples who among them wanted to live with him in Paradise after his death. What might be the reason, many people of Jesus' time also believed God raised him up to heaven before he was crucified. It is the reason God has said in the Quran that He has left the matter of Jesus' crucifixion to the assumption of people, but made the hostile Jews believe that it was Jesus who was crucified.

With this testimony in the Quran, we also know for certain that Jesus didn't die on the Cross for the sin of mankind as most of his devoted followers claim about him.

God testifies through Muhammad that Jesus also asked his people to get rid of their sin through sincere repentance

The Quran tells us that Jesus also asked his people to get rid of their sin through sincere repentance as did all his predecessors before him, or as did Muhammad who was sent after him. Truth can be checked first in the following statements of the Quran.

Evidence from the Quran

: He that seeks guidance shall be guided to his own advantage, but he that goes astray does so to his own loss. No bearer shall bear the burden of another on the Day of Judgment. (17:15)

: If anyone does evil or wrongs his own soul but afterwards seeks Allah's forgiveness, he will find Allah Oft-Forgiving, Most Merciful. (4:110)

: Seek the forgiveness of your Lord and turn to Him in repentance. (11:3)

: Your Lord is indeed Forgiving and Merciful to those who do something wrong through ignorance but later repent and rectify their ways. (16:119)

: Your Lord knows best what is in your hearts. If you do good deeds, certainly He is most forgiving to those who turn to Him again and again in true repentance. (17:25)

: O My slaves who have transgressed against their souls, do not despair of Allah's mercy, for Allah forgives all sins. Truly, He is the Oft- Forgiving, the Most Merciful. Turn in repentance to your Lord and submit to Him before the torment comes upon you when you will find none to help you. (39:53)

Both parts of the Bible also teach the same to the people how to get rid of their sin

Evidence from the Old Testament

: Parents are not to be put to death for their children, nor children be put to death for their parents; each will die for their own sin. (Deut. 24:16)

: The one who sins is the one who will die. The child will not share the guilt of the parent, nor will the parent share the guilt of the child. The righteousness of the righteous will be credited to them, and the wickedness of the wicked will be charged against them. (Eze. 18:20)

: Therefore, you Israelites, I will judge each of you according to your own ways, declares the Sovereign LORD. Repent! Turn away from all your offences; then sin will not be your downfall. (Eze. 18:30)

: Turn from evil and do good; then you will dwell in the land forever. For the Lord loves the just and will not forsake his faithful ones. (Psalm 37:28-29)

: The righteousness of the perfect shall direct his way: but the wicked shall fall by his own wickedness. (Pro 11:5)

Evidence from the Gospel of Jesus

: But go ye and learn what that meaneth, I will have mercy, and not sacrifice: for I am not come to call the righteous, but sinners to repentance. (Matt. 9:13)

: Jesus answered, "Do you think that these Galileans were worse sinners than all the other Galileans because they suffered this way? I tell you, no! But unless you repent, you too will all perish. (Luke 13:2-3)

: Or those eighteen who died when the tower in Siloam fell on them-do you think they were more guilty than all the others living in Jerusalem? I tell you, no! But unless you repent, you too will all perish. (Luke 13:4-5)

God testifies through Muhammad that Jesus also asked his people to seek for their eternal life through keeping His commands

The Quran tells us that God's guidance for all of mankind to return to Him as their ultimate Refuge began with their parents Adam and Eve when they ate the forbidden fruit from the Garden of Eden by the instigation of Satan. But God forgave them when He saw the couple to repent for their sin sincerely and to beg Him for His mercy and forgiveness.(7:23) Then before they were sent to earth along with Satan as their open enemy, God said to them:

"Get down from here all of you, henceforth there shall come to you guidance from me; and those who accept and follow it shall have nothing to fear or to regret. But those who reject and defy our revealed guidance will be inmates of hellfire, where they shall live forever." (2:38-39)

Since then God began sending His guidance to the people through their respective messengers which finally ended with Prophet Muhammad-the last and the final of them. But the bottom line in the guidance of God as we have noticed in both our scriptures-the Quran and the Bible, has always remained the same. It is, man should strive for their eternal life through keeping the commands of God. I have quoted some of them first from the Old Testament of the Bible, then from the Quran and finally from the Gospel of Jesus.

Evidence from the Old Testament of the Bible

Moses, the mighty Messenger from the House of Israel, asks his people pleading,

"Hear, Israel, and be careful to obey so that it may go well with you and that you may increase greatly in a land flowing with milk and honey, just as the LORD, the God of your ancestors promised.

: Hear, O Israel: The LORD our God is one LORD. Love the LORD your God with all your heart, and with all your soul and with all your strength." (Duet 6:3-5)

: Fear the LORD your God, serve him only and take your oath in his name. Do not follow other gods, the gods of the people around you. (Duet 6:13-14)

" Honor your father and your mother....You shall not murder. You shall not commit adultery. You shall not steal. You shall not give false testimony against your neighbor. You shall not covet your neighbor's house. You shall not covet your neighbor's wife, or his male or female servant, his ox or donkey, or anything that belongs to your neighbor." (Exodus 20:12-12-)

" Ye shall diligently keep the commandments of the LORD your God, and His testimonies, and His statutes, which He hath commanded thee. (Duet 6:17)

"And observe what the LORD your God requires: Walk in obedience to him, and keep his decrees and commands, his laws, and regulations, as written in the Law of Moses. Do this so that you may prosper in all you do, and wherever you go." (1Kings 2-3)

Evidence from the Quran

: We gave him [Abraham] Isaac and Jacob and guided them all as we guided Noah before them, and among his descendants were David, Solomon, Job, Joseph, Moses and Aaron; thus, We reward those who do good to others.

: Other descendants include Zechariah, John, Jesus, and Elias; all of them were righteous. and Ishmael, Elisha, Jonah, and Lot. We exalted each of them over mankind. And we exalted some of their forefathers, their children, and their brothers. We chose them for Our service and guided them to the Right Path. (6:85–87)

: We gave Moses the Book [Torah] and made it a guide to the children of Israel commanding: Take not other but Me as the Disposer of your affairs. (17:2)

[God says to Moses]: "I have chosen you. So, listen to what I reveal to you. Verily, I am Allah: There is no God but Me. So, worship Me alone and establish regular prayer for my remembrance." (20:13-14)

: Then, in the footsteps of those prophets, We sent Jesus, the Son of Mary, confirming the Law [Torah] that had come before him: And We sent him the Gospel where there was guidance and light and confirmation of the Torah which was sent before him; a guidance and admonition to those who fear Allah. (5:46)

: Your Lord has decreed to you that: you shall not worship none but Him, and you shall be kind to your parents; if one or both attain their old age in your lifetime , you shall not say to them any word of contempt nor repel them and you shall address them in kind words.(17:23)

: O believers! Stand firm for justice and bear true witness for the sake of God, even though it goes against yourselves, your parents, or your relatives….. If you distort your testimony or decline to give it, then you should remember that God is fully aware of your actions. (4:135)

: You shall not commit adultery, surely it is a shameful deed and an evil way. You shall not kill any one whom God has forbidden, except for just cause. (17:32-33)

…..those who commit evil and become encircled in sin are the inmates of hellfire. As for those who believe in God and do good deeds, they will be the residents of Paradise. (2:81-82)

Evidence from the Gospel of Jesus

Jesus-the last Prophet of God from the House of Israel, says to his people:
"Do not think that I have come to abolish the Law or the prophets; I have not come to abolish them but to fulfill them. For truly I tell you, until heaven and earth disappear, not the smallest letter, not the least stroke of a pen, will by any means disappear from the Law until everything is accomplished. Therefore, anyone who sets aside one of the least of these commandments and teaches others, accordingly, will be called least in the kingdom of heaven, but whoever practices and teaches these commands will be called great in the kingdom of heaven. (Matt. 5:17–19)

:And, behold, one came and said unto him, Good Master, what good thing shall I do, that I may have eternal life?

:And, he said unto him, Why callest thou me good? There is none good but one. That is God: but if thou wilt enter into life, keep the commandments. (Matt. 19:16-17)

I hope no explanation is required to understand the message of those verses that I quoted above from the Quran, the Old Testament of the Bible and finally from the Gospel of Jesus. Both the Scriptures tell us clearly to worship none but One God, to repent for our sin, and to strive for our eternal life through keeping the commands of God.

I shall now try to explain other prophecies of Jesus that he made about his Comforter, meaning Muhammad to show my readers how he fits with each of them without having any question or confusion.

In John 14:26, Jesus said to his disciples: "But the Comforter, the Holy Spirit, whom the Father will send in my name, will teach you all things, and remind you of everything I have said to you."

While explaining Jesus' prophecy in John 15:26-27, I already mentioned that Muhammad's name has been mentioned *paracletos* in the Greek version of the Bible and it was translated in English as advocate, comforter, counselor, friendly, or 'one being sought for help. But many of my Christian Missionary friends believe the Comforter in the quoted prophecy is meant for the Holy Spirit who was Archangel Gabriel, though they failed to provide any valid evidence in support of their claim. But the Muslims have many valid reasons to claim Jesus' Comforter was Prophet Muhammad whom he meant to come after him to remind his people of what they forgot from his teaching. Let me explain first from both the Bible and the Quran why the Holy Spirit doesn't match with any part of Jesus' prophecy but Muhammad does.

From the narration of the Bible and the Quran we have learned that the job of the Angel Gabriel was to convey the words of God to His designated messengers on earth and to help them to carry out their prophetic mission. But nowhere in the Bible or in the Quran the Holy Spirit was mentioned to teach the people anything or to remind them of what the messengers of their time taught them. Most important of all, Jesus has made it clear to his disciples that his Comforter would come after he leaves, while both the scriptures tell us the Holy Spirit used to come to Jesus and his mother during their lifetime. Truth can be checked in the following verses of the Gospel as well as in the Quran.

The angel answered, "The Holy Spirit will come on you [Mary] and the power of the Most High will overshadow you...(Luke 1:35)

....and the Holy Spirit descended on him (Jesus) in a bodily form like a dove. (Luke 3:22)

:Then Allah will ask: "O Jesus, son of Mary! Recall my favor upon you and to your mother, how I strengthened you with the Holy spirit." (Quran 5:110)

At this point, my Christian friends would like to know why Jesus said the Comforter was the Holy Spirit, if he was not? The answer is Jesus meant Muhammad as the Holy Spirit. Let me provide evidence from both the Gospel and the Quran in support of that.

The Holy Spirit in this prophecy (John 14:26) refers to Muhammad-the last Prophet of God

In the following statement of the Gospel the *Spirit* has been used for both true and false prophets.

Dear friends, "do not believe every spirit but test the spirits to see whether they are from God because many false prophets have gone out into the world. This is how you can recognize the Spirit of God: Every spirit that acknowledges that Jesus Christ has come in the flesh is from God, but every spirit that does not acknowledge that Jesus Christ has come in the flesh is not from God." (1John 4:1–3)

In the quoted statement *the spirit* has been substituted for a prophet from humankind regardless of his status. In other words, John-a disciple of Jesus didn't mean any angel or a spiritual being to tell us whether Jesus came to the world in the flesh or not. He meant a true Prophet of God would come from humankind to remind the world who Jesus really was and why he was sent for.

John also pointed out how to differentiate a true prophet of God from the false one. A true Prophet would never say that God has appeared to them in the flesh of Jesus, but a false prophet would claim so. A true Prophet of God would also tell them that Jesus was a man of flesh and blood, and he was sent to guide his people to the Path of God. It is what Muhammad did when God sent him after Jesus along with His last guidebook-the Quran. I shall now try to explain the last part in John 14:26 where Jesus said, "*He will teach you all things and will remind you of everything I have said to you.*"

"He will teach you all things and will remind you of everything I have said to you," describes Muhammad accurately

Being an inspired Messenger of God, Jesus knew in advance that a day would come after him, when his followers would be misled by the invented doctrines of men and forget what he taught them by the command of God. At the same time, Jesus also knew that God would send His Last Prophet Muhammad along with His final Scripture-the Quran reminding them of everything that he taught them himself and what he never taught. I already described it while explaining Jesus' prophecy in John 15:26-27. Instead of repeating that, we may now check what Jesus predicted about Muhammad in John 16:13. He said to his disciples:

"When he, the Spirit of truth, comes, he will guide you into all the truth. He will not speak on his own; he will speak only what he hears, and he will tell you what is yet to come."

I don't need to explain *the spirit of truth* because I already have done it while explaining Jesus' prophecy about his Comforter in John 15:26-27. I will only try to explain how the remaining parts of the quoted prophecies also apply to Prophet Muhammad without any strain.

"He will guide you into all truth," refers to none but the last Prophet

In this part, Jesus informed his disciples that when *the Spirit of truth* meaning Muhammad would come after him, he would guide them into all truth. To understand this part clearly, I need to explain first what Jesus has meant by *all truth.*

By *all truth* Jesus meant the essence or the spirit in the commands of God that He sent through all His messengers beginning from Adam to His last Prophet Muhammad. It is pure and pristine monotheism where God is claimed to be One and Only and no one in the entire heavens and earth is worthy of worship besides Him. Abraham received it as the everlasting covenant of God (Gen. 17:7); while Moses and Jesus received it as the First Commandment of God. (Duet 6:4-5; Mark 12:29-30).

Muhammad who arrived nearly six hundred years after Jesus, mentioned it as *Tawhid* [in Arabic] meaning the absolute oneness and the supremacy of God over everything in the universe and none has any right to be worshiped except Him. It is also called 'Islamic monotheism' because Islam is the only religion on earth where the basic truth in the guidance of God, which is pure and pristine monotheism, has remained intact and uncontaminated until now.

According to the report of Merriam-Webster's Encyclopedia of World Religions, "Islamic monotheism is more literal and uncompromising than that of any other religion. Allah is confessed being one, eternal, unbegotten, unequaled, and beyond partnership of any kind." [page 747]

Being an inspired Messenger of God, Jesus knew that Muhammad will be sent after him reviving and reinstating the monotheistic faith of all his predecessors in Islam. Based on that inspired knowledge from God, Jesus said to his disciples when the Comforter meaning Muhammad would arrive after him, he would guide them back to the eternal truth of the First Commandment which he preached and practiced himself when he was with them. It happened so as he predicted. The history of religion also tells us Muhammad is the only Prophet of God until now who came after Jesus along with the Quran reminding his misled followers and all of mankind repeatedly that God is One and to worship none but Him.

We may now check the next part of the prophecy in John 16:13, where Jesus said,

"He will not speak on his own; he will speak only what he hears."

This prophecy of Jesus also applies to none but Prophet Muhammad. To verify the truth of my claim, I need to inform my Christian friends how the words of the entire Quran were revealed to him.

According to the well-established Islamic Tradition and the authentic biographies of Prophet Muhammad, we also came to know that when he reached his age forty, he began meditating in the solitary cave of Mount Hira in Makkah-the city of his birth. During one such night in the month of Ramadan [9th month in the Arabic calendar] Archangel Gabriel appeared to him with some words from God and asked him to read. As Muhammad was illiterate and did not know how to read or write, he had to repeat the words of God with the Angel until he committed them by heart completely and correctly. Then he delivered those words to his people as he heard and learned from the Angel. In other words, while delivering the words of God, he did not add anything of his own, nor he omitted or held back anything from what the Angel of God conveyed to him. Thus, he began receiving and teaching the words of God in the same manner for the last twenty-three years of his life as a Prophet of God.

The Holy Quran which we read today still carries the same words as Muhammad received from God through His Angel Gabriel more than fourteen hundred years ago. In that case, it is very much expected that Jesus meant the illiterate Prophet Muhammad who said nothing on his own but said only what he heard from the Angel of God. The Quran also testifies that Muhammad only conveyed those words to his people which he received from God (46:9; 10:15) There are other verses in the Quran where Muhammad was warned to be punished if he dared inventing any word in the name of God (69:43-46)

At this point, I would also like to remind my readers that through fulfilling this prophecy of Jesus, Muhammad also fulfilled God's Promise to Moses about sending a Prophet like him in Deut. 18:18, where He said: "I will raise them a Prophet from among their brethren, like unto thee, and will put my words in his mouth; and he shall speak unto them all that I shall command him."

Muslims believe that prophet is Muhammad because he conveyed the words of God to the people as he was commanded to do in the Quran. But the Bible and other scriptures before the Quran do not contain the exact words of God. They also contain the words of the prophets and even the words of the ordinary people. In this context, I would also like to remind my readers that Muhammad also fulfilled the prophecy of Isaiah who mentioned him being unlearned or illiterate (29:12) and how the entire Quran was revealed to him. (28:10-11)

I narrated those prophecies in detail in my book ANNA ASKED WAS MUHAMMAD A PROPHET? [Her question is answered from The Bible and other major scriptures of the world]

We may now check how the last part of Jesus' prophecy in John 16:13 also matches with the Arab Prophet Muhammad without any question.

"He will tell you what is yet to come," also matches with Muhammad without any question

By this prediction Jesus meant that like many other prophets of God, Muhammad would also make prophecies, and they would also come true in course of time. To check the truth of this prophecy of Jesus, we need to know first about those prophecies of Prophet Muhammad which he made more than fourteen hundred years ago.

According to the narration of many authentic Hadith [traditions related to Prophet Muhammad's words and deeds as reported by his close companions] he made a series of prophecies on various subjects or issues. Now we know some of them occurred in his lifetime. Some of them occurred soon after his demise, while many of them have still been occurring in and around us, proving the sanctity of his message and mission as a true Prophet of God. Out of his countless prophecies, I have stated below only a few of them.

- Muhammad's prophecy on the Roman's victory over the Persians became true in his lifetime.
- The day before the battle of Badr, Prophet Muhammad said to his companions mentioning the names of some of his pagan enemies and showing the places in the field of Badr where they would be killed by the Muslims. So it happened as he said.
- During his illness at the end of his life, Muhammad called his daughter Fatima to his bedside and told her she would be the first among his family to join him after his death. So, it happened. Fatima, who was then only twenty-eight, joined her father only six months after he left.
- Muhammad predicted the caliphate [the reign of his rightly guided four Caliphs after his death] would last for thirty years, and then there would come a biting kingship. The history of Islam tells us this prophecy of the noble Prophet Muhammad also became true, as he said.
- Muhammad predicted Uthman [third Caliph of Islam] would be killed while reading the Quran. So, it happened.
- Muhammad said to his close companions that they would conquer Egypt, Damascus, Jerusalem, Iraq, Persia, Constantinople, and Cyprus. All those places were conquered by them after he left.

The Prophet also made the following prophecies the truth of which is now more than evident.

- The barefooted Bedouins would compete in building tall buildings, and the mosques would look like palaces.
- Killing would increase in such a way that the one who killed would not know why he killed, and the one killed would not know why he was killed.
- Sexual promiscuity would increase, and a new disease, which people had not heard of before, would spread among them because of that.
- Women would appear naked while still being dressed.
- People would hop between cloud and earth (refers to journey by plane).
- Islam would reach as far as the remotest corners of the world in the East and the West and it would enter every house on earth.

Besides those prophecies, Muhammad also predicted about the Signs of the Last Hour and Jesus' Second Coming. We believe all of them will come to pass according to the pre-set timetable of God.

We may now check another prophecy of Jesus in John 16:14 where he said: *"He shall glorify me: for he shall receive of mine and show it unto you."*

This prophecy of Jesus also describes Muhammad accurately. Let's see how. Many of my Christian friends might wonder how Muhammad who arrived nearly six hundred years after Jesus, could glorify him. They will find the answer in the Quran, the last and the final guidebook of God. There are many verses in the Quran where God has raised the name and the status of Jesus and his mother Mary high forever through His last Prophet Muhammad. For example, God has established the truth of Jesus' virgin birth in the Quran through His last Prophet Muhammad and thus made him and his mother free from the slander of the Jews.

Similarly, God also made Jesus free from the accountability of those invented doctrines of men which his followers still believe and practice in his name after he left. (3:42-47; 19: 27-30; 4:156-58, 5: 46, 72-73, 75, 110; 10:68; 19:88-92; 21:91; 43:59) I already described them while explaining Jesus' prophecies in John 15:26. Since no one came yet to glorify Jesus other than Prophet Muhammad, we may rightly claim it is Muhammad whom Jesus meant to glorify him. We may now check another prophecy of Jesus where he said:

"Nevertheless I tell you the truth; It is expedient for you that I go away: for if I go not away, the Comforter will not come unto you; but if I depart, I will send him unto you." (John 16:7)

By this prediction, Jesus made it clear to all that he did not mean the Holy Spirit or the Angel Gabriel to come after him because the Gospel also tells us he used to visit not only Jesus but also his mother Mary before his birth.

> And the angel came in unto her, and said, Hail, thou that art highly favoured, the Lord is with thee: blessed are thou among women. (Luke 1:28)
>
> And the Holy Ghost descended in a bodily shape like a dove upon him, which said, thou art my beloved son; in thee I am well pleased. (Luke 3:22)

In that case, it is understood that Jesus' Comforter will be a chosen person of God who would arrive after he leaves. As far as we know, Muhammad was the only Prophet of God in the history of religion who was sent after Jesus with the same prophetic mission as his. We can also accept it as a valid evidence that Jesus' Comforter was Muhammad whom he meant to come after him to glorify and testify of him and to remind his followers of what they forgot from his teaching and above all, to guide them back to the eternal truth of the First Commandment which they forsook and began to follow the invented doctrines of men after he left.

"Another Comforter" is Prophet Muhammad whom Jesus meant to stay with his followers forever

In John 14:16, Jesus made another prophecy about his Comforter where he said to his disciples:

"And I will pray to the Father, and he shall give you another Comforter, that he may abide with you forever."

We shall try to examine first what Jesus really meant by *another Comforter*. The scholars of the Bible used the Greek word *allon* for another. It also means "another of the same kind." Based on that meaning or implication, we can rightly assume that Jesus wanted for his followers *another Comforter* like him. It means he will also be a Prophet like Jesus, and he will also call them to believe in One God, to worship none but Him and to strive for their eternal life through keeping His commands as he did when he was with them.

We shall now try to know what Jesus meant in the last part of his prophecy where he said to his disciples *that he may abide with you forever*.

At this point, many of my Christian friends may ask in wonder how

Muhammad, who came long after Jesus with a different scripture and a different religion, could live forever with his followers. My answer is Jesus meant his true followers are those who follow what he has left for them in his teaching or in the instances of his life. But looking at the faith and practices of his devoted followers, it is more than evident that they have deviated from his teaching completely when they imposed divinity upon him and made him an object of worship along with God.

In that case, it is very much expected that Jesus meant the Muslims as his true followers who never deviated from the eternal truth of the First Commandment which God revived through Prophet Muhammad in Islam and made it a way of life for all of mankind. We shall now check how Jesus' Comforter Muhammad has remained alive forever with his followers meaning the Muslims through some valid and verifiable evidence from both Islamic and non-Islamic sources.

Islamic Sources

Muhammad will live forever through his Sunnah meaning the set examples of his life

The believers in God and in their life Hereafter, are repeatedly asked in the Quran that they must follow the *sunnah* of Prophet Muhammad meaning the ways or the practices of his life that he has left for them. The Quran also tells us that the followers of the Prophet's sunnah, will obtain immense reward, mercy and forgiveness from God. I have quoted below some of them for my non-Muslim readers.

: Say, [O Muhammad], "If you love Allah, then follow me, Allah will love you and forgive your sins. And Allah is Forgiving and Merciful. (3: 31)

: He who obeys the Messenger [Muhammad] has obeyed Allah; but I have not sent you over them as a guardian who have deviated from His Path. (4:80)

: There is certainly an excellent pattern for you in the Messenger of Allah [Muhammad] who believes in Allah and the Last Day, and who remembers Him often. (33:21)

: O you who have believed, obey Allah and obey the Messenger [Muhammad] and do not invalidate your deeds [through your disobedience to them] (47: 33)

: O you who have believed, fear Allah and believe in His Messenger [Muhammad]; then He [God] will give you double portion of His mercy and make for you a light by which you will walk, and will forgive you…(57: 28)

Based on the contents of those Quranic verses, all the practicing Muslims meaning the true followers of Muhammad have taken him as their role model and try to live their daily life by his *Sunnah* meaning the set example of his life that he practiced himself following the guidance of the Quran. It means they try to do all the important chores of their personal, family, social, professional, political, religious or spiritual life following the *Sunnah* of the Prophet. In this way, he has remained alive in the practices of his true followers as their role model and he will remain so until the end of the world proving the truth of what Jesus has said about him.

Muhammad's name is remembered aloud ten times a day

Muhammad's name is remembered aloud ten times a day in all Muslim countries as well as in the Muslim-populated areas of the world through the *Adhan* of a *Muezzin*. *Adhan* is to call the Muslims aloud to attend their five times daily obligatory prayers through some prescribed words in Arabic. And *Muezzin* is a caller who makes that call from a local masjid or a place of worship. They usually make that call about fifteen minutes before the prayer begins. Among those prescribed words in the *Adhan* there is a part the meaning of which is, "I witness that there is no God but Allah," and the next part is, "I witness that Muhammad is the Messenger of Allah,".

The Muezzin announces both the parts twice five times a day. At this point, I also like to remind my non-Muslim friends that *Adhan* has become an indispensable part of Islamic rituals since the time of Prophet Muhammad. We do not know any other Prophet of God before Muhammad whose name has been attached or announced with God as His Messenger ten times a day. They may feel amazed to know that the Muslim are also required to utter each part of the *Adhan* along with the *Muezzin* when they hear it, and at the end of *Adhan* they also need to ask God to bestow His peace and blessing upon Prophet Muhammad and to place him in the highest level of Paradise. If half of the Muslims from nearly 2 billion of them [based on the current report of the Pew Research Center] listen to *Adhan* and witness Muhammad as the Messenger of God and ask Him for His mercy and blessing upon Muhammad five times a day, it is understood how many times a day he is remembered by his followers.

In this context, I also like to inform my Christian friends that Muslims are also required to testify Muhammad as the Servant and Messenger of God and to ask God for His peace, mercy, and blessing upon him fourteen times a day while saying their five times daily obligatory prayers. Along with those obligatory prayers, they also make many optional and special prayers every day and throughout the year, and all their prayers will remain incomplete and unacceptable, if they do not testify Muhammad as the Messenger of God or ask God to bestow His peace, mercy, and blessing upon him. It is for their knowledge and information, I also like to mention that to become a Muslim and to remain a Muslim, they are also required to say, *"I testify there is no God but Allah, and I also testify that Muhammad is the Servant and the Messenger of Allah."*

A moment does not pass when Muhammad's name is remembered aloud or in silence

Remembrance of Muhammad's name aloud or in silence becomes more intensified and incessant in both Makkah and Medina-the place of his birth and demise, and especially during the time of Hajj or the Big Pilgrimage once a year in Commemoration of Abraham's sacrifice his son near Makkah where millions of Muslims attend to observe it from all over the world.

At this point, it is also important to note that the Muslims are also required to invoke God for His peace and blessing upon Prophet Muhammad every time they utter, hear, read, or write his name.

We also have no clue how many thousand tons of books have been written so far on various aspects of Muhammad's life only by the Muslim writers to keep his name alive forever in the history of mankind.

In fact, a moment does not pass on the surface of earth when his followers do not ask God to send His mercy and blessing upon their beloved Prophet Muhammad.

At this point, it is also interesting to note that a current poll shows the name "Muhammad" has surpassed all other names used by men. We may now check how Muhammad will live forever among his followers from the non-Islamic sources.

Non-Islamic Sources

Muhammad will also live forever in the writing of the non-Muslim scholars

My Christian friends may know it or not, but it is also a fact that Muhammad will live forever in the writings of the non-Muslim scholars, especially the open-minded scholars of the Western world. I have quoted below some of their observations or assessment about Muhammad from their writings in support of that.

I like to begin with the observation of Edward Gibbon-the famous historian and scholar of Europe in the late eighteenth century. In his book *The History of the Decline and the Fall of Roman Empire* (1776), he says:

"The Creed of Muhammad is free from the suspicion of ambiguity and the Koran is a glorious testimony to the unity of God. The Apostle of God submitted to the menial offices of the family, he kindled the fire, swept the floor, milked the ewes, and mended with his own hands his shoes and garments."

Thomas Carlyle-a renowned Scottish philosopher, historian, and a writer paid a rich tribute to Prophet Muhammad in his famous book *Heroes and Hero-Worship and the Heroic in History* (1840), where he said:

"A silent great soul, one of that who cannot but be earnest. He was to kindle the world-the world's Maker has ordered so.

A false man founded a religion. Why, a false man cannot build a brick house! ...It will not stand for twelve centuries [it is more than fourteen centuries now] to lodge a hundred and eighty million [nearly 2 billion today, the second largest on earth] it will fall straight away"

Rev. Bosworth Smith, an American Protestant Episcopal Bishop, and the author of *Muhammad and Muhammadanism* (London 1874), describes:

"He (Muhammad) was a Caesar and Pope in one; but he was Pope without the Pope's pretentions, and Caesar without the legions of Caesar: without a standing army, without a bodyguard, without a palace, without a fixed revenue; if ever any man had the right to say that he ruled by the right Divine, it was Muhammad, for he had all the powers without its instruments and without its supports."

John William Draper, MD, LLD, was a professor of Chemistry and Physiology and a distinguished writer of many valuable books on the inconsistencies and the conflict in history and religion. In his book- *A History of the Intellectual Development of Europe* (London 1875), he said:

"Four years after the death of Justinian, A.D. 569, was born in Mecca, in Arabia, the man who, of all men has exercised the greatest influence upon the human race…To be the religious head of many empires, to guide the daily life of one-third of the human race, may perhaps justify the title of a Messenger of God."

In his valuable book-*Histoire de la Turquie* (Paris, 1854), Alphonse de Lamartine-a famous French scholar wrote in appreciation of Muhammad:

"If greatness of purpose, smallness of means and astonishing results are the three criteria of human genius, who could dare compare any great man in history with Muhammad? The most famous men created arms, laws, and empires only. They founded, if anything at all, no more than material powers which often crumbled away before their eyes. This man moved not only armies, legislations, empires, peoples, dynasties, but millions of men in one-third of the then inhabited world; and more than that, he moved the altars, the gods, the religions, the ideas, the beliefs, and the souls… the founder of twenty terrestrial empires and of one spiritual empire that is Muhammad. As regards all standards by which human greatness may be measured, we may all ask, is there any man greater than he?"

We may now check what George Bernard Shaw- a renowned Irish author, a playwright, and a Nobel Prize winner thought of Prophet Muhammad and his religion Islam. In his book *The Genuine Islam* (Vol. 1, No. 8, 1936), he said:

"I have studied him-the wonderful man-and in my opinion far from being anti-Christ, he must be called the savior of humanity. I believe that if a man like him were to assume the dictatorship of the Modern world, he will succeed in solving its problems in a way that would bring to it the much-needed peace and happiness."

"If any religion had the chance of ruling over England, nay Europe within the next hundred years, it could be Islam. I have always held the religion of Muhammad in high estimation because of its wonderful vitality. It is the only religion which appears to me to possess that assimilating capacity to the changing phases of existence which can make it appeal to every age………"

Jules Masserman- an American Jew, a renowned psychoanalyst, and a professor at Chicago University, also found Muhammad to be the greatest of all leaders. In his essay published in *Time* magazine on July 15, 1974, he said that leaders must fulfill three functions-provide for the well-being of those being led, provide a social organization in which people feel relatively secure, and provide them with one set of beliefs.

People like Louis Pasteur and Jonas Salk are leaders in the first sense. People like Gandhi, Confucius, Alexander, Caesar, and Hitler are leaders in the second sense and perhaps in the third sense. Jesus and Buddha belong in the third category alone. Perhaps the greatest leader of all times was Muhammad, who combined all three functions. To a lesser degree, Moses did as well.

Interestingly, the history of the World also tells us Prophet Muhammad achieved this unparalleled achievement in the field of religion, in running the administrative affairs in most parts of the Arab world, and in changing a barbaric and unruly nomad of the desert into a disciplined, organized and a morally and spiritually oriented nation only in the last ten years of his life after he became a Prophet of God at his age forty.

I intend to end this part with the observation of Michael Hart-an American author and astrophysicist. In his book -*The 100, A Ranking of the Most Influential Persons in History* (Carol Publishing Group: New York, 1989), he reported:

> "My choice of Muhammad to lead the list of the world's most influential persons may surprise some readers and may be questioned by others, but he was the only man in history who was supremely successful on both the religious and secular levels. ... Muhammad founded and promulgated one of the world's great religions and became an immensely effective political leader. Today, 13 centuries (nearly 14 and a half now) after his death, his influence is still powerful and pervasive. .... It is the unparalleled combination of secular and religious influence which I feel entitles Muhammad to be considered the most influential single figure in human history."

The Muslims believe it is that single figure in the history of mankind, whom Jesus meant to come after him to testify and glorify him, and to guide his misled followers to the eternal truth of the First Commandment which they eventually forgot and forsook after he left.

Despite those crystal-clear instances and evidence that I narrated so far mostly from the Gospel and the writings of the non-Muslim scholars, if my Christian friends still hesitate to accept Muhammad as Jesus' Comforter, or they like to think that Jesus meant someone else who didn't arrive yet, I'd humbly ask them to read and reflect upon a few prophecies more that I am going to present to them from both parts of the Bible-the Book they claim themselves as the true words of God.

CHAPTER TWO

THE PROMISED PROPHET IN DEUT 18:18 IS JESUS' COMFORTER MUHAMMAD

Frankly speaking, there are countless prophecies in both parts of the Bible containing the arrival of Jesus' Comforter Muhammad whom he meant to come after him as his testifier and a guide to the truth. (John 15:26; 16:13) I have tried to narrate them in detail with evidence and explanation in the previous chapter. In this chapter, I intend to present an oft-quoted statement from the Book of Deuteronomy where God has said to Moses:

: I will raise them a Prophet from among their brethren, like unto thee, and I will put my words in his mouth; and he shall speak unto them all that I shall command him. (Deut 8:18)

While explaining a prophecy of Jesus about his Comforter in John 16:13, I already have described in the previous chapter how the last part of the quoted statement which is *I will put my words in his mouth; and he shall speak unto them all that I shall command him*, fitted Muhammad perfectly. So, I will skip that and explain only the first part of the statement where God has said to Moses, *I will raise them a Prophet from among their brethren, like unto thee.*

The Christians claim *that Prophet* is Jesus while the Muslims claim he is Jesus' Comforter Muhammad whom he meant to come after him. (John 16:7). Both have also provided reasons to justify their claim.

The Christians say Jesus was like Moses because both were Jews, and they belonged to the same House of Israel. In that case, both Moses and Jesus were brothers to each other.

They say like Moses, Jesus also received the words of God and conveyed the same to his people as did Moses before him.

Their other important reason is Muhammad was a non-Jewish Arab, and therefore he could no way be a brother of Moses who was a Jew.

Muslims-on the other hand, say the Christians somehow forget that all the prophets of the Bible who came after Moses, were like Moses because all of them were Jews and belonged to the same tribe. In that sense, Jesus was not alone; all the prophets of the Bible who were sent after Moses, were like him.

They also say that all the true prophets of God used to convey the words of God to their people as they were commanded to do. In that case, Jesus was not alone, all the chosen prophets of God were like Moses.

Muslims do not consider Jesus as Moses' brother because like Moses he also belonged to the same House of Israel and therefore, he should be considered as one of them.

Besides those points, Muslim also have many valid reasons to justify the promised Prophet in Duet. 18:18, is not Jesus but his Comforter Muhammad whom he mentioned to come after him as his testifier, glorifier, a guide to the truth and a reminder of what he taught his people being commanded by God. We shall first try to know why the Muslims believe Jesus is not like Moses, but Muhammad is.

Why Jesus is not like Moses, but Muhammad is

First, Jesus was born to Virgin Mary which means his birth was not normal, but unusal or miraculous. But both Moses and Muhammad were born to a married couple.

> Then said Mary unto the angel, how shall this be, seeing I know not a man? And the angel answered and said unto her, The Holy Ghost shall come upon thee, and the power of the Highest shall overshadow thee.
> (Luke 1:34-35, KJV)
> "O my Lord! How shall I have a son when no man has touched me?" He (the angel) replied, "Even so, Allah creates what He wants. Whenever He decides to do anything, He only says to it, "Be," and it is," (Quran 3:47)

Second, Jesus never married, but both Moses and Muhammad did.

Third, the Christians claim Jesus as the only begotten Son of God, God Incarnate, and as one of the Gods in the Trinity, but the followers of both Moses and Muhammad believe they were only the messengers of God and their job was to guide their people to the Path of God.

Fourth, Jesus is believed to die on the Cross for the sin of mankind and for their eternal life in heaven, but Moses and Muhammad made no such sacrifice for their people, except teaching them to strive for their eternal life through keeping the commands of God.

Fifth, the Christians believe Jesus was resurrected from death on the third day, but both Moses and Muhammad have remained buried in their graves since they died.

Sixth, the Christians believe Jesus went to hell and remained there for three days to compensate for their sin, but Moses and Muhammad did not take any such trouble for the sin of their people, except telling them that they are accountable for their own sin and they need to do to redeem their sins through repentance and keeping the commands of God.

Seventh, the Christians believe Jesus ascended to heaven alive and he would return to earth to establish for them the promised kingdom of God. But the role and the mission of both Moses and Muhammad as the designated prophets of God have ended with their death.

Eighth, both Moses and Muhammad were accepted, obeyed, and respected by most of their people as the chosen Messengers of God in their own lifetime. But the Gospel tells us Jesus' own people-the Jews rejected him as a Messiah of God.

> He (Jesus) came unto his own, but his own received him not.
> (John 1:11, KJV)

Ninth, both Moses and Muhammad were accepted by their people not only as the mighty Messengers of God, but also as their kings or supreme heads though they never sat on the throne in any imperial robes, or with a crown on their heads. But like the Roman, Egyptian, or Persian emperors, both had absolute power and authority over every field in the administration. Jesus on the other hand, said: *My kingdom is not of this world.* (Jn. 18:36) In other words, Jesus opted only for the spiritual world while Moses and Muhammad tried to build a material as well as a spiritual world for their people.

Tenth, both Moses and Muhammad were sent with a set of divine laws to maintain peace, justice, and security for their country and people. But the Gospel tells us that Jesus was sent to implement the laws of the Torah-the Book that Moses received from God for the guidance of his people. (Matthew 5:17-19) The Quran also tells us that Jesus was sent with the Gospel with guidance and light and confirming the Law of the Torah. (5:46)

We may now check how Muhammad also fulfilled the next part of the prophecy in Dt. 18:18 where God said to Moses that He would send that Prophet *from among their brethren*, meaning from the brothers of the Israelite.

The Promised Prophet of God would arrive from the brethren of the Israelite

In Jewish language and culture, all full-brothers, half-brothers, even the cousins with a distant family tie are called brothers or brethren without making any discrimination among them. Based on that Jewish family Tradition, we shall now check how Muhammad-the non-Jewish Arab Prophet became a brother of the Jewish Prophet Moses. To find their link or connection, we need to go back to Prophet Abraham whom God addressed as the father and the leader of many nations in both Bible and Quran.

Genesis-the first Book of the Old Testament tells us about Abraham and his first wife Sarah, who was barren, and what happened after she made her husband marry Hagar, her Egyptian handmaid for the sake of children. They will find that description in chapter 16 and 21 in the Book of Genesis. I need to narrate that story briefly for them who are not aware of it.

When Hagar found she was pregnant with Abraham's child, she began to despise Sarah- her mistress and co-wife. Sarah naturally felt very annoyed and insulted. She told her grievances to Abraham, who permitted her to deal with her maid as she pleased. Abraham gave that permission because he knew according to the law of the country, Sarah had absolute ownership over Hagar as her slave. But the situation got worse for expecting Hagar when Sarah-her mistress and co-wife, began to deal with her as she really pleased. Her pleasure caused her maid so much pain that she couldn't bear it anymore. One day she ran away from home. After she travelled a long way, she sat down by a fountain being exhausted and aggrieved. It was then God appointed an Angel to take care of her and to send her back to her mistress Sarah.

The Angel also told Hagar she was carrying a son and God chose his name Ishmael. Then he advised her to go back to Sarah and she listened to him probably thinking of her son's wellbeing and safety. When Ishmael was fourteen years old, God blessed Abraham with Isaac through his barren wife Sarah, keeping His promise that He made to Abraham one year ago. Now the bottom line is Abraham had two sons from his two wives, and both were obviously brothers to each other.

Hagar and Ishmael were abandoned near Kabah-the Sacred House of God at Makkah

After the birth of Isaac, Sarah somehow found many excuses not to let her son grow up with Ishmael-his big brother. In the weaning ceremony of Isaac, she asked her husband to abandon his son Ishmael along with his mother. Abraham found it very grievous, but he fulfilled her wish being commanded by God. Next morning Abraham gave them some bread and a bottle of water before they began their walk to an unknown land. Hagar made her journey along with her son Ishmael through the wilderness of Paran. When the bottle of water became empty, Hagar feared the death of her son and began to cry by the side of a bush. At that time, the same Angel of God appeared to her once again and helped them to survive and settle by the well that God had sprouted for them (Gen 21:8-21).

It is now discovered that Mount Paran was in the valley of Baca or Bakka (Psalm 84:6), now called Makkah. The Islamic Tradition also tells us that it is the place where the remains of Kabah-the Sacred House of God at Makkah remained hidden in a mound. It is the same place where Ishmael grew up under his mother's care and supervision, became a good archer, and then took a wife from the tribe of Jorham who settled with them later. Ishmael had twelve sons and one daughter. It is also from the progeny of Ishmael's second son Kedar arrived Muhammad-the last and the final Prophet of God.

The Book of Genesis also describes that Ishmael's younger brother Isaac settled with his parents in Hebron near Jerusalem and both the brothers were known to maintain their family-ties. After Abraham died, both of his sons buried him together (Gen 25:9). Jacob's son Esau was also known to marry the daughter of Ishmael-the elder brother of his grandfather Isaac (Gen 28:9).

From the history of the Semitic religion and culture, we also have learnt that people who came from the lineage of Isaac are called Israelite. But this title was not given to them after the name of Isaac. It was given after the name of Jacob whom God named Israel (Gen. 35:10). Similarly, people who came from the lineage of Ishmael are called Ishmaelite. Thus, both the Israelite and the Ishmaelite became cousins or brothers to each other. I hope now it is clear to all how the non-Jewish Arab Prophet Muhammad fits perfectly with the prophecy in Deut 18:18 where God says to Moses, *I will raise them a Prophet from among their brethren.*

If they need more evidence to accept Ishmael-Abraham's firstborn as the Progenitor of Prophet Muhammad, I will ask them to read the following prophecy from the Book of Isaiah:

> And there shall come forth a rod out of the stem of Jesse, and a branch shall grow out of his roots: And the spirit of the LORD shall rest upon him, and the spirit of wisdom and understanding, the spirit of counsel and might, the spirit of knowledge and of the fear of the LORD. (Isa 11:1-2)

In this statement, the "rod" or the "branch" refers to a man who would arrive from the stem or the trunk of Jesse, meaning from the lineage of Jesse. In that case, to identify the man, we need to identify first who that Jesse was? Before I go into that, I like to point out the Christians believe as usual this prophecy is meant for Jesus. They believe so because they have learned from the Book of Matthew that Jesus came from the lineage of David, whose father was Jesse. But some well-reputed scholars of the Bible, both Christians and non-Christians, old and modern, questioned its validity for three important factors.

First, according to the genealogy in the first chapter of Matthew, Jesus was mentioned as the son of David. But nowhere in the Bible Jesus was called the son of Jesse or he came from Jesse.

Second, David's father Jesse had no mentionable rank or position. In that case, it does not sound appropriate that his name should be taken into consideration as Jesus' forefather.

Third, it sounds very unlikely that Jesus, who was born without a human father and described in the Gospel as the child of the Holy Ghost (Matt 1:18), would ever need to be linked with an unknown and ordinary person to determine his lineage. With these questions in mind, the open-minded scholars of the Bible-both Christians and non-Christians, began to trace the rod of Jesse from other sources.

Jesse came from *Yishay*, which is the abbreviation of Ishmael-Abraham's firstborn

While exploring the root of Jesse in the Hebrew Bible, they discovered Jesse came from *Yishay* (pronounced yee-shah-ee) or from *Iyshay* in Aramaic (pronounced ee-shah-ee), which is the abbreviation of Yishma'el (pronounced yish-maw-ale)-Abraham's firstborn. But when a popular trend developed with the European translators to replace the Y for J, the name *Yishay or Iyshay* changed into Jesse. The Encyclopedia Biblica also tells us Jesse has been contracted or abbreviated from Ishmael (vol.3, p. 3292, item 52).

The rod that came out from the stem of Jesse is Muhammad-the last Prophet of God

Based on that information it is now more than evident that the rod mentioned in the prophecy of Isaiah refers to Muhammad- the last and the final Prophet of God. My Christian friends may feel amazed to know that Muhammad is the only Prophet of God who arrived from the progeny of Ishmael-Abraham's firstborn.

The last part of Isaiah's prediction also matches perfectly with the dispositions of Muhammad's conduct or character. The open-minded scholars of all religions who studied Muhammad's life and achievements, informed us how the spirit and the strength of his character, the depth of his wisdom and understanding, the merit of his advice or counseling, and above all the integrity of his faith along with his fearful and complete submission to the will and the command of God, made him the most adorable and extraordinary human being on the surface of the earth. I already mentioned about his unparalleled achievement and influence in both religious and secular fields while explaining a prophecy of Jesus in the previous chapter.

We may now consider another prophecy from the Book of Isaiah to confirm Jesus' Comforter was Muhammad-the last Messenger of God whom he meant to come after him as his testifier.

In Isa. 9:6, we are told:

> For unto us a child is born, unto us a son is given: and the government shall be upon his shoulder and his name shall be called Wonderful, Counselor, the mighty God, the everlasting Father, the Prince of Peace.

Many of my Christian missionary friends believe as usual this prophecy is meant for Jesus, because the first part of the prophecy has mentioned about the birth of a son. From my long association with my Christian missionary friends, I have noticed their unquestioning faith in Jesus' being the only begotten and beloved Son of God and because of that it never occurs to their mind that the *son* can also be applied to another chosen person of God. I think it might be the only reason they took the birth of *a child or a son* in the above-quoted statement for Jesus, though other parts of the prophecy do not match with him at all. We shall first try to see why other parts of the prophecy do not apply to Jesus but apply to the Arab Prophet Muhammad perfectly.

Why other parts of the prophecy in Isa. 9-6, do not apply to Jesus but apply to the Arab Prophet Muhammad

The *child* or *son* does not apply to Jesus because the prophecy also tells us *the government shall be upon his shoulder,* which indicates the *child* or the *son* would one day hold the highest or the topmost position in the administration of his country. In other words, he would run the government of his country as the supreme head. This part of the prophecy does not apply to Jesus at all, because nowhere in the Gospel Jesus is mentioned holding any official post-big or small in the administration of his country. Not only that, when Jesus was arrested by the Roman soldiers on the false charge of sedition, he admitted himself to the governor Pilate that his kingdom was not for this world (Jn. 18:36). But this prophecy applies to the Arab Prophet Muhammad perfectly because the history of Islam tells us he ruled over a large part of Arabia not only as the Supreme Head, but also as an extraordinary political leader, social organizer, lawmaker, dispenser of laws, warrior, and a commander-in-chief in the last ten years of his life after he declared himself a Prophet of God at his age forty.

The last part of the prophecy in Isa 9:6 also describes Muhammad accurately

While explaining the name of Muhammad as Jesus' Comforter or Advocate in the previous chapter, I have narrated the meaning and implication of "Muhammad" in both English and Greek. Let me repeat what I said before. When translating Muhammad's name from Hebrew or Aramaic to Greek, the translators used two names *periclytos* and *paracletos*. Of these two Greek names, *periclytos* corresponds directly to the meaning of the Prophet's Arabic name Muhammad, which is praise, praiseworthy, desire, desirable, adorable, altogether lovely.

But some translators of the Bible from Greek to English, chose the name *paracletos* which has been retranslated as comforter, advocate, wonderful, counselor, kind, friendly, or 'one being sought for help.' Interestingly, this meaning also describes Muhammad perfectly, because people of his time also knew him as a kind, comforting, and a friendly person whom they constantly sought for help, advice, or counsel long before he claimed himself a Prophet of God. As no other recognized prophet of God is known to have the name Muhammad with the similar meaning or implication, we may consider rightly that this part of the prophecy in Isa. 9:7, is meant for the Arab Prophet Muhammad whom God sent after Jesus as his testifier.

We shall now check the last part of the prophecy where the *son* or the *child* is called *prince of peace*. The Christians always feel delighted to call Jesus as *The Prince of Peace* and besides him, they could think of none who could also deserve that title. I think they call him so probably without knowing what Jesus said about himself in the following statements of the Gospel.

Jesus said he didn't come to bring peace on earth but division

Jesus said to his disciples in Matt. 10:30-34,

"Do not suppose that I have come to bring peace on earth, I did not come to bring peace, but a sword. For I have come to turn a man against his father, a daughter against her mother, a daughter-in law against her mother -in law."

In Luke 12:51-53, Jesus asked his disciples,

"Do you think I came to bring peace on earth? No, I tell you but division. From now on there will be five in one family divided against each other, three against two, and two against three. They will be divided, father against son and son against father, mother against daughter and daughter against mother, mother-in-law against daughter-in-law, and daughter-in-law against mother-in-law."

Jesus' declaration of his coming to earth not to bring peace but to bring division among the close members in a family, may shock most of his devoted followers. They might wonder how Jesus, who said to love their enemies and to pray for those who persecute them (Matt. 5:44), and who commanded them to love their neighbors as they love themselves, and to consider it next to loving God (12:30-31); could declare so openly that he came to destroy the bondage of love and unity among the close members of a family! Frankly speaking, I also felt the same when I read those statements for the first time. Then I understood it was a kind of metaphoric expression where Jesus left for his followers an inherent message rather than its apparent meaning. Let me explain with evidence.

Being an inspired Messenger of God, Jesus knew in advance about the arrival of some false prophets with their invented doctrines to deviate his followers from the eternal truth of the First Commandment after he leaves. Jesus also knew how his devoted followers would be tortured, persecuted, and forced to worship him as God or as one of the Gods in the Trinity in place of One True God. As the deviation from his teaching would take place in his name, and the division among the close members of the family was bound to happen in consequence of that, Jesus out of his own humility and frustration describes it as his own doing. There are many authentic and well-documented books on Jesus' life and teaching as well as on the persecution in the early churches which tell us why this persecution took place and how it shook the very foundation of his followers' faith and families after he left.

Similarly, being an inspired Messenger of God Jesus also knew about the arrival of Prophet Muhammad along with the Quran-the last Scripture of God proclaiming the worship of none but One True God among the unruly and uncivilized polytheists of Arab, and to establish peace, justice and unity among them by implementing the laws of God as He has described in the Quran. So, it happened when Muhammad was sent after Jesus fulfilling his prayer and prediction both. The truth can be checked not only in the history of religion, but also in the history of the world where we shall find how Muhammad-an illiterate Arab Prophet changed the arrogant, ignorant, corrupt, hostile and the lawless pagans of the Arabian deserts into a God-fearing, truth-seeking, law-abiding, disciplined, and morally and spiritually oriented nation only in the last ten years of his life after he began ruling them as the head of the state.

I like to invite my readers to read the next and the last chapter of this book where I intend to provide more evidence from the Gospel to justify my claim that Jesus' Comforter was Muhammad-the last and the final Prophet of God.

CHAPTER THREE

"That Prophet" in John 1:19-21, is Jesus' Comforter Muhammad

In John 1:19-21, we find an interesting conversation between John-the Baptist and the Levites who arrived from Jerusalem. The Quran has mentioned John the Baptist as Prophet Yahyaa, who was born to Prophet Zachariah at his very old age. The Quran also says John was sent before Jesus confirming his arrival as the Word of God [meaning the creation of Jesus by His commanding word "Be"]. (3:39, 59)

We shall now examine the following conversation in between John-the Baptist and the Levites and then try to figure out why the Muslim claim *that prophet* in their conversation refers to none but the promised Prophet of God in Deut 18:18, meaning the Arab Prophet Muhammad whom Jesus mentioned as Comforter in John 14:26; 15:26; and 16:7.

> And this is the record of John, when the Jews sent priests and Levites
> from Jerusalem to ask him, who art thou?
> And he (John the Baptist) confessed I am not the Christ.
> And they asked him, what then? Art thou Elias?
> And he said I am not.
> Art thou that prophet? And he answered, no. (John 1:19-21)

From their conversation, we understand that the Jews were aware of the arrival of Christ, the re-arrival of Prophet Elias [also called Elijah] and of *that prophet* whom they did not know by name or title but knew of his arrival from God's promise to Moses in Deut 18:18. While explaining that prophecy in the last chapter, I already have mentioned how each part of God's promise to Moses became true through Muhammad-the last and the final Prophet of God. Since no prophet arrived yet other than Muhammad, we may rightly assume *that prophet* in John 1:19-21 refers to none but Muhammad whom God has sent after Jesus fulfilling his prayer and prediction both. At this point, my Christian friends may want to know about the arrival of Elias/Elijah whom the Jews were also expecting to come before Jesus. We shall come to that, after I clarify certain points concerning the arrival of Elijah/Elias.

It is, if we claim *that Prophet* was meant for Muhammad, who arrived nearly six hundred years after Jesus' ascent to heaven, the question of Elijas' second coming remains unanswered, because we do not come across any prophet of God by the name Elijah or Elias before Jesus except John-the Baptist. When the disciples of Jesus asked him about Elijah's arrival before him (Matt. 17:10), he replied to them:

"To be sure, Elijah comes and will restore all things. But I tell you, Elijah has already come, and they did not recognize him, but have done to him everything they wished. In the same way the Son of Man is going to suffer at their hands." Then the disciples understood that he was talking to them about John the Baptist. (Matt.17:11-13)

Jesus confirms John the Baptist was Elias /Elijah

From his reply they understood that Jesus meant John-the Baptist because by this time, they also came to know how he was imprisoned and beheaded by King Herod to please the whims of a woman whom he loved (Mark 6:14-16).

At this point, we may feel confused to think why John the Baptist said to the Jews he was not Elias when they asked him straight, but Jesus said to them he was? The believers in God usually believe the true prophets of God never lie or cheat and they try to do everything as they are commanded by God. In that case, any sensible person would like to know why John-the Baptist replied to the Jews he was not Elias, but Jesus said he was?

We need to find the answer using our own intelligence and common sense. It is possible John was not aware that he was Elias. Or if he knew, he did not want to disclose his identity to them being inspired by God. Maybe, God wanted the Jews to know about him through Jesus as they knew about Jesus through him. But whatever the reason is, Jesus confirms to the Jews that Elias or Elijah has already arrived by the name John fulfilling their expectation.

Muhammad in the prophecy of John the Baptist

In this context, we may check another prophecy made by John-the Baptist in Mt. 3:11 where he said:

I indeed baptize you with water unto repentance: but he that cometh after me is mightier than I whose shoes I am not worthy to bear, he shall baptize you with the Holy Ghost, and with fire.

Muslims believe this prophecy was meant for Muhammad, though the Christians believe as usual it was meant for Jesus. They believe so without considering the meaning or implication of all its parts which do not apply to Jesus. For example, the Gospel tells us John has arrived before Jesus, and he used to baptize people with water and through repentance. Jesus also did the same when he arrived after John. But in his prophecy, John said the one who would come after him would be mightier than him, and he was not worthy to bear his shoes. Let me explain first what made the Muslims think John did not mean Jesus to be mightier than him. They think so from a statement of Jesus where he said:

: Verily I say unto you, among them that are born of women there has not been a greater than John the Baptist (Mt 11:11).

The message in the above-quoted statement has made it clear that John-the Baptist did not mean Jesus to be mightier or greater than him, or he was not worthy to bear his shoes. Considering the phenomenal achievement or success of Prophet Muhammad both in religious and secular fields, we may rightly assume that it is Muhammad whom John meant mightier or greater than him. The Quran also tells us Muhammad was the best ideal for them who believe in God and in the next life, and remember God much. (33:21) We shall now check the last part of John's statement where he said: 'he shall baptize you with the Holy Ghost, and with fire.'

The Prophet who will baptize people with the Holy Spirit and with fire, is Jesus' Comforter Muhammad

We shall now try to understand how Muhammad fits that description perfectly. From the contents of the quoted verse, we came to know that the Prophet whom John-the Baptist meant to come after him, wouldn't baptize people with water as he did or as did Jesus. But he would baptize them with the Holy Ghost/Spirit and with fire. I already have described in the first chapter about the role and mission of the Holy Spirit/Ghost meaning the Archangel Gabriel.

From the narration of both Bible and Quran, we have learned the Holy Spirit used to convey the words of God to all His designated messengers on earth and to help them to perform their prophetic jobs among their people. In many places of the Quran as well in the Islamic Tradition, we are also told how the Holy Spirit also assisted Muhammad to face, fight and defeat his pagan opponents who were three times large in number, provision, weapons and were more competent in war-skill than his. Finally, with the help of the Holy Spirit, Muhammad was able to defeat them and establish the worship of none but One True God among the Arab pagans who were in general ignorant, arrogant, unruly, hostile, and barbaric in nature. Not only that, he also changed them into a God-fearing, truth-seeking, and law-abiding-nation in the last ten years of his life with the guidance of the Quran that he received from God through the archangel Gabriel. So, John-the Baptist was right when he said the man who would come after him, he would baptize people with the Holy Ghost/Spirit.

We shall now check what John meant by baptizing people with fire. Fire usually stands for warfare, which became a part and parcel in Muhammad's life against the pagans of Makkah since he declared himself a Prophet of God and began to call them to worship none, but One God as did all his Predecessors before him. But they rejected his call and began to oppose him vehemently. Based on the narration of the Quran, Islamic tradition and the history of religion, we also came to know that they also started humiliating and torturing the Prophet and his followers inhumanly. Finally, when they planned to kill the Prophet, he migrated to Medina and so did many of his followers before and after him.

After Muhammad settled in Medina, he had to fight many battles with his deadly enemies of Makkah. With his limited source and power, he fought with those who were well-equipped, well-trained, well-provisioned, and much larger than his army. But finally he defeated them all with the help of the Holy Spirit and a band of angels that God sent for his assistance. It is also a recorded part in the history of mankind how Muhammad won Makkah with his ten thousand saintly followers without any fight, declared amnesty to all, and brought the pagans of Makkah under the shade of Islam only eight years after his migration to Medina. Both parts of the Bible and other major scriptures of the world also predicted this phenomenal victory of Prophet Muhammad against the pagans of Makkah.

After this victory, Muhammad also tried to rectify and enlighten their heart and soul by the teaching of the Quran that he received from God through the Holy Spirit Gabriel. He also encouraged them to take part in *Jihad,* meaning the holy war to establish the worship of One God and His laws, to defend their homes and countries, and to ensure peace, security and justice for all. He also taught them that their lives, blood, and possessions given in *Jihad* would purify them from their sins and assure them eternal life in heaven. If by baptism, we mean to bring a change in the hearts of men with the love, light, or the spirit of God, it was undoubtedly Prophet Muhammad and his devoted followers who brought that change in the mindset of the unruly and barbaric Arabs through sacrificing their lives, blood and all their possessions purely for the sake of God. I hope my readers will now understand what John-the Baptist really meant when he said the man who would come after him would baptize people with fire. In that case, Jesus could no way be that Prophet because he used to baptize people only with water and through repentance.

Jesus said, "The kingdom of God will be taken from you and given to a people who will produce its fruits." (Matt. 21:43)

I intend to end the topic of my discussion with another prophecy of Jesus where he said: *The kingdom of God will be taken from you and given to a people who will produce its fruits.* (Matt. 21:43)

In this prediction Jesus meant Palestine as the kingdom of God which was then run by the House of Israel meaning the Jews and the Christians. He also said it will be given to the people of another nation who will make it productive or useful. Though Jesus didn't spell out clearly why it will be taken away from them, or who was that nation whom it will be given, it is understood.

The history of the world tells us the other nation is the Muslim or the companions of Prophet Muhammad who conquered it at the time Omar al-Khattab, the second Caliph of Arabia and made it a peaceful abode for them and for the people of the House of Israel meaning the Jews and the Christians both. This other nation who began to spread through Muhammad-the progeny of Ishmael-Abraham's firstborn has also been mentioned in several places of the Old Testament of the Bible. (Gen 16:10; 17:20; 21:13, 18; Isa. 11:1-2)

There is also a verse in the Quran where God has said He has given them [the people of Israel] Book, authority, and prophethood. But if they deny it, then it will be given to a nation who will not deny it. (6:89)

Truth can also be checked in the History of Semitic religion and culture how Jesus' prediction became true after Muhammad arrived fulfilling his prayer and prediction both. (John 14:16)

Before I end this topic, I would like to request all my Christian and non-Christian friends to read my book ANNA ASKED WAS MUHAMMAD A PROPHET? where I have tried to provide more prophecies on Muhammad's advent not only from the Bible but also from other major scriptures of the world sent before the Quran.

CHAPTER FOUR

Some Interesting Questions That I Faced After I Published My Book

I needed to add this chapter for those readers who might have the same or similar questions as one of my Christian missionary friends asked me after I presented her a copy of my book ANNA ASKED WAS MUHAMMAD A PROPHET? [Her question is Answered from Bible and other major scriptures of the world] when it was published first by the Toplink Publication. I still thank her gratefully for her questions because it gave me another chance to provide more evidence to clarify the sanctity of Muhammad's role and mission as the last and the final Messenger of God for all of mankind.

One late morning on Saturday, I was visited by Miss Gilbert-one of my old and orthodox Christian missionary friends. She was in her middle age. Besides her nursing job, she also worked as a missionary on her off days. She was a devout Christian, soft-spoken, and straight forward while talking about her faith in Jesus. I also knew she had lots of reservation to accept Muhammad as a true prophet of God and the Quran as His Final Testament for all of mankind. Despite that, I liked to talk to her only to know more about Jesus whom we love and believe as a unique and a special Messenger of God from the House of Israel. I also gave her a copy of my book with the hope that she might accept Muhammad as the last Prophet of God if she knew what the prominent Prophets of the Holy Bible, especially Jesus, had said about his advent along with his role and mission.

So, I welcomed her happily and sat together in my prayer cum study room. I felt a bit excited when I found her taking out the copy of my book from her handbag which I presented to her on her last visit about two weeks ago. I instantly thought she read my book and now she was going to appreciate me for writing this book and for letting her know the truth about Muhammad. But she surprised me by saying sweetly, "Sorry, I couldn't complete your book. I only read the first few pages. Then I felt I needed a bit of clarification to some of my questions before I start reading your book seriously."

"Sure. If it is within my knowledge, I'll certainly try to answer your questions. So, tell me frankly what you want to know?"

"Thanks a lot." She said delightfully and then said sweetly, "I've four questions. First, I would like to know why you, I mean the Muslims are so eager to tell the people of other faiths what their scriptures have said about Muhammad?

"My second question is, do they need the support of other non-Muslims to establish Muhammad's claim as the last Prophet of God?

"I'm also interested to know whether they, I mean the Muslims want to establish the superiority of the Quran over all other scriptures of the world?

"And my last question is whether they want to establish the superiority of their religion Islam over all other religions of the world?"

Frankly speaking, I didn't expect any of those questions from her at that moment. I also didn't understand why she needed the answers to those questions to read my book seriously? I felt so disturbed and disheartened that I wanted to tell her to return my book and to leave. But I tried to ignore my frustration and decided to answer all her questions with some verses from the Quran. I thought it might help her to find the truth and to accept Muhammad as the last Prophet of God.

With this intention in mind, I said to her, "Thanks for your questions, Miss Gilbert. I hope you will bear with me until I answer all your questions one by one."

"Sure."

"Thanks."

Why the Muslims are so eager to tell the people of other faiths what their holy scriptures have said about Muhammad?

"In reply to your first question," I began telling her very politely and choosing my words carefully, "I like to admit frankly that as a Muslim I want to inform all my non-Muslim readers, especially the Christians what their Holy Scriptures have really said about Muhammad.

"May I please know why, especially the Christians?"

"Because I feel myself one of them since I began to live here with them as a citizen of this country. The other important reason, the Quran also tells us that like the Jews and the Christians, Muslims also have inherited their monotheistic faith from Abraham. Maybe, it is for that long and deep-rooted link or heritage of our faith, I felt myself very much connected with them. So, when I came to know that like most of the Jews the Christians also rejected Muhammad as an imposter, it was then I thought I should tell them what their Holy Bible has said about Muhammad's arrival along with his role and mission. I believe you'd have done the same if you were in my place. Wouldn't you?

Do the Muslims need their support to justify Muhammad's claim as the last or the final Prophet of God?

Without waiting for her answer I continued, "In reply to your second question, my answer is obviously no. I mean Muslims do not need anyone's support or feedback to establish Muhammad's claim as the last or the final Prophet of God. Because God took care of that Himself. Let me justify my point with a brief statement from the Quran."

Then I picked up the meaning of the Quran in English by Marmaduke Pickthall from the coffee table and opened chapter 33 and read to her verse 40 where God has said: *Muhammad is not the father of any man among you, but he is the Messenger of God and the Seal of the Prophets.*

After I finished reading, I began to explain, "According to the description of the authentic biographies of Prophet Muhammad, he fathered three sons, but all of them died during their childhood. In other words, Muhammad had no male inheritor to call him father or to carry on his prophetic mission after him.

"If you think," I said to her lightly, "Muhammad made this statement himself after the death of his three sons, I'd then ask you to check the last part in the verse where he has been declared as the "Seal of the Prophets." It means Muhammad was the last of all prophets and no prophet would be sent after him.

Not only that, by this declaration God also made it clear to all that the legacy of His revelation has also been ended with Muhammad. The truth of this statement is now more than evident. Because we do not know any prophet of God to arrive with a Book like the Quran or a religion like Islam in the last fourteen hundred years. Doesn't it confirm that Muhammad is the last and the final Prophet of God as it is said in the Quran, the Bible and in other major scriptures of the world?"

Do the Muslims want to establish the superiority of the Quran over all other scriptures of the world?

In her silence, I continued, "Now, let me come to your third question. The answer is again no. I mean, Muslims don't need to establish the superiority of the Quran over all other scriptures of the world, because God has taken care of that, too. Let me explain to you how. There is a brief verse in the Quran where God has said He has certainly revealed the guidance, and He will certainly protect it from all corruption. (15:9)

"To verify the truth of this Quranic statement, you may examine several copies of the Quran in the Arabic text printed or published from anywhere in the world regardless of the date of their publication. You don't have to know Arabic to check the truth. You may check them as the little kids identify similar letters or words from their worksheets. You will find the words in each verse of the Quran have remained the same as they were delivered to to Prophet Muhammad more than fourteen hundred years ago.

In this context, I also like to inform you that the original languages of other sacred texts have largely been extinct or lost. Besides that, many transgressions were also made in them by the people of vested interest either through deleting the words of God or adding something new to it to serve their purpose. Do you think the sanctity of the Quran could be saved like this for so many centuries, if it were not protected by God Himself?"

Do the Muslims want to establish the superiority of Islam over all other religions of the world?

"In reply to your last question," I said, "My answer also remains the same which is no. I mean Muslims don't need to establish the superiority of Islam over other religions of the world, because God took care of that, too. I will try to justify my claim with a verse from the Quran. Then I picked up the meaning of the Quran in English by Muhammad Farooq-i-Azam Malik from the side table and read to her verse 9 from chapter 61.

: It is He Who has sent His Messenger with the guidance and the religion of truth so that he may proclaim it over all religions, much as the polytheists may dislike it.

"In this verse," I began to explain, "He" obviously refers to God and "Messenger" to His last Prophet Muhammad. Then the "guidance" that God has sent through Muhammad certainly refers to the Quran- His last and final guidebook and "the religion of truth" that Muhammad received from God to proclaim over all other religions of the world, is undoubtedly Islam. Then I said to her, being very humble and polite, "I think, I don't have to explain to you who the polytheists are, right?"

"Yes, they are the people who worship idols." Mrs. Gilbert said in brief.

"Not only them, anyone who worships God in association with others, is also a polytheist. We may now check the truth in the declaration of God which I just read to you. You may be surprised to know that this declaration in the Quran goes hand in hand with the current projected data of the Pew Research

Center. The report tells us if Islam maintains its current rate of growth without any interruption, meaning without facing any natural or manmade disaster, the number of its adherents which is now nearly 1. 9 billion, will be the largest on the planet by the end of this century when one out of the three people will be a Muslim. Interestingly, this data is also going to fulfill a prophecy of the Arab Prophet Muhammad who said Islam would reach every home on earth.

"I think," I said to her after a few moments of silence, "I have tried to answer all your questions with some valid and verifiable evidence to establish Muhammad's status as the last or the final Prophet of God as it is said in the Quran and in other major scriptures of the world including the Bible. If you want to check the truth you can read those scriptures, or you can read my book to save your time."

"I'll certainly read your book from cover to cover, I promise." She looked serious and concerned.

"Thanks a lot Miss Gilbert. Please feel free to ask me any questions after you read my book."

"Sure. Remain safe and blessed till then."

"Same to you." I began walking to the door with her after she picked up the copy of my book from the table and put it in her side bag.

: Those who follow the Messenger, the unlettered Prophet, whom they find mentioned in the Torah and the Gospel, who enjoins upon them what is right and forbids them what is wrong and makes lawful for them what is good and prohibits for them what is evil and relieves them of their burden and the shackles which were upon them. So, they will be successful who will believe in him, honor him, support him and follow the light, which is sent down with him. (Quran 7:157)

BIBLIOGRAPHY

1. Abdullah Mishaal Ibn, What Did Jesus Really Say? Ann Arbor, MI 48105, Islamic Assembly of North America, 1996.
2. Ali, A. Yusuf, The Holy Quran Text, Translation and Commentary. Brentwood, Maryland, Amana Corp. 1983.
3. Badawi, Jamal, Muhammad in the Bible. Cairo, Egypt: Al Falah Foundation for Publication and Distribution, 2005.
4. Deedat, Ahmed, What the Bible Says About Muhammad Durban, South Africa: IPCI, 1993
5. Glasse, Cyril, The Concise Encyclopedia of Islam. New York: Harper Collins, 1991.
6. Jerald F. Dirks, Abraham the Friend of God, Amana Publications, Maryland, USA, 2002
7. Kalby, Kais, Prophet Muhammad the last Messenger in the Bible. USA, 2005
8. King James Versions Nashville, Thomas Nelson Publishers, 1977.
9. Maulana Abdul Haque Vidyarthi, Muhammad in World Scriptures, Dar-ul Kutub Islamia, Lahore, 1940.
10. Merriam-Webster's Encyclopedia of World Religions. Springfield, Massachusetts, 1999.
11. Muhammad Alamgir, Muhammad in the Vedas And Puranas, 50704 Kuala Lumpur (translated from its Bengali Version by Prof. Asitkumar Bandopaddhaya from its original Hindi transcript by Dr. Ved Prakash Upapaddhaya), 1998
12. New Revised Standard Versions, The Harper Collins Study Bible, Harper SanFrancisco.
13. New International Version Published by Zondervan, Michigan, USA, 2011
14. Pickthal. Muhammad M. The Holy Quran with Arabic Text, & English Translation, Delhi: Kutubkhana Ishayat-ul-Islam.
15. Sayd Ashfaque Ullah, Index of Qur'anic Topics. Washington D. C Amana

Publications for the IFTA Office, 1999.

16. Shafi Muhammad Mufti, Maariful Quran, Islamic Foundation, Dhaka, Bangladesh, 1983.

17. Siddiqui, Faisal, The Bible's Last Prophet. Alexandria, VA, AlSaadawi Publications, 1995.

ABOUT THE AUTHOR

Dil R Banu, a Muslim by birth and practice, and a retired Lecturer from a prestigious College of her Homeland Bangladesh, settled in Maryland more than thirty years ago. She worked as a substitute teacher in the local elementary school for a year and then began to operate a licensed family daycare in her rented apartment where most of her neighbors were Christians. This job was a turning point in her life because it made her a writer from a daycare provider. During this period, many Christian missionaries used to visit her. The main purpose of their visit was to inform her how she could get rid of her sin and have eternal life in heaven through having faith in Jesus. While talking to them on this issue from her point of faith, she understood they had many reservations to accept Muhammad as a true Prophet of God and because of that, they also had many misconceptions about his religion Islam and about the teaching of the Quran which he claimed to receive from God. But she became truly surprised to know many elites, scolars, and even the well-known evangelists of the Christian world also belong to them. It was then she decided to write this book to help them find out the truth about Muhammad from their own Bible-the Book they claim to contain the true words of God.

She learned from the Quran, the Bible, and other major scriptures of the world that the eternal truth in the guidance of God and in the teaching of all His prophets beginning from Adam to His last Prophet Muhammad, is pure and pristine monotheism where God is claimed to be One, Eternal, and none has any right to be worshiped except Him. She also believes peace and justice for all of mankind cannot be achieved until pure and pristine monotheism is established on earth thoroughly and completely in their faith and practices.

ABOUT THE BOOK

The title of the book has made it clear about its contents and why it has been written. The people of all faiths especially the devoted followers of Jesus Christ who are truly confused about the role and mission of Muhammad-the last and the final Prophet of God, might reshuffle their thoughts and look at him differently, if they know what Jesus has said about his advent in the Gospel-the Book they claim themselves as a true account of his own words and deeds.

A review on the author's first book
ONE GOD FOR ALL

By Rae C. Bernard

There is always a comparison and contrast to both spiritual texts, between the Bible and the Quran, on whose God is better or most powerful. Surprisingly, the debate will forever remain between Judeo-Christians and Muslims, until both sides become more open-minded to the possibility of a One God, no matter what name is preferred for reference. In One God for All, author Dil R. Banu ensures readers that God is one in the same regardless of what another religion, specifically of Islam are calling Him, by providing evidence from both spiritual texts. People are always trying to prove there is a difference between what they believe versus others they encounter and this book demonstrates otherwise. By reading this book, you'll gain a level of open mindfulness. Maybe, there is more than what you've been raised or taught to believe. You learn that the text in both the Quran and the Bible share unexpected similarities, especially for someone who has never read both books of spiritual texts.

Jesus and Muhammad are the most important individuals in each book because they are the last of God/Allah's messengers for the people on earth. One would be fascinated in learning that both messengers were created to fulfill similar purposes. This grants the ability to step outside of your in-box thinking and consider the proof provided to you, encouraging the overall goal of a One God for everyone. Of course, one would think because there are different books, there would be different views on what's believed and it's not the case with this book. Not once has the author critiqued or opted to project her views onto the readers, setting the reading experience in more of an educational tone.

The author used letters as a method to educate readers, which shows various correspondences with a reverence about specific Holy Scriptures. This enables clarity for those assuming that the beliefs of Muslims are not the same as those of Judeo-Christians. Personally knowing Jesus was the created son brought down by God to provide a sacrifice for His people, was interesting to learn that Muhammad had a similar role. It is a true eye-opener discovering that prophets and messengers had a particular task to aid the evolving world and its inhabitants. Either beliefs want its people to remain on a righteous path, following the rules/commandments of God/Allah or it's up to each individual to uphold their end of the agreement.

I've never had the opportunity to read the Quran in my entire life, I was amazed by the way their text had instances like the Bible. In learning this, I started to come to understand just how strong the Islamic beliefs are and why they seem hardcore to do anything in the name of Allah. I felt that I can take away quite a few scriptures from the Quran that are in agreement with the Bible and know that they too want the same thing for their lives and their people. I am very appreciative of the author for delving into both books and finding Scriptures from each to aid her case that we all believe in One God, and only one alone. The book is well-written with personal research, spending time in gathering the proper evidence to provide clarity to readers. I highly recommend anyone who wants to discover for themselves just how similar both spiritual books can be to consider reading One God for All, as the author saved her readers time and the necessity for having to read both.

A review on the author's second book

ANNA ASKED WAS MUHAMMAD A PROPHET?

[Her question is answered from Bible and other major scriptures of the world]

By Aaron Washington

Author Dil R. Banu first started by defining what prophecy is. I was impressed with her detailed explanation as it made me have a deeper understanding of the definition and why God's people are referred to as prophets. There are so many people who claim to be prophets in today's world. This can be confusing to believers who follow anyone who proclaims the word. The author further expounded on the subject of false prophesy with a Bible verse (Duet 18:21-22). Through that verse, we learn the true prophets make correct prophesies, but it is God who inspires them. False prophets, on the other hand, rely on their imagination, making them fail most of the times.

Dil R. Banu's intent when writing Anna Asked Was Muhammad a Prophet was to show the link between Muhammad and the prophets in the Bible. Christianity and Islam may operate on a different basis, but the fact remains that there are some fundamental beliefs in both the Quran and the Bible which link the two. This is what the author wants everyone to understand. Anna Asked Was Muhammad a Prophet is a religious book which helps even the unobservant and least interested readers know more about religion and Prophet Muhammad. It is amazing how the author broke everything down. I learned much about Islam teachings vis-a-vis the Christian gospel by the end of my read.

One of the most fascinating parts in the book was when the author explained the relation between Muhammad, Jesus, and Moses. Contrary to popular belief, Muhammad was not like Jesus. He was more like Moses. This is because Jesus was born of the Virgin Mary, in a miraculous way. Both Moses and Muhammad, however, were born to a married couple. The two later got married and had their own offspring. The next comparison between Moses and Muhammad versus Jesus was that the two were accepted, obeyed, and respected by most of their people as the true messengers of God in their own lifetime. This was not the case with Jesus. Jews rejected Jesus and his mission and even claimed that he was not the true Messiah. Dil R. Banu's discussion of the three brought about a lot of clarity to this history. At the end of the day, I was able to tell the three apart and noted the roles they played.

Reading Anna Asked Was Muhammad a Prophet gave me the impression of going through the Bible and the Quran simultaneously. The author did a fantastic job by writing this book as it helped me have a better understanding of the two books. Dil R. Banu's book is nothing short of informative. The author is engaging too and wrote from an informed point of view. Other than her way of explaining things, I have to mention the author's choice of words was another thing that made this book easy to read. The language used is simple, with the exception of a few technical words which are well outlined in the text. This book is ideal for a wide range of reading audiences from early adult on up, and of virtually any faith, with any degree of religious background.

A review on the author's third book
ABRAHAM WAS COMMANDED TO SACRIFICE ISHMAEL-HIS FIRSTBORN

By Md Mahbubur Rahman, Ph.D.

Anna Asked, Was Muhammad a Prophet? is an appealing exploration of religious history and theological inquiry that investigates deeply into the lives and legacies of key biblical and Quranic figures. The book addresses a profound question posed by the author's friend, Anna, about the prophet Muhammad, and it thoughtfully examines the intersections of Judaism, Christianity, and Islam.

The author begins by recounting her close friendship with Anna, which provides a heartfelt and personal backdrop to the book. Their age and ethnic differences only deepen their bond, highlighting the universal nature of their inquiry. The question that sparked the book—about Muhammad's prophetic status leads the author into a broader exploration of another contentious issue: which of Abraham's sons was intended for sacrifice.

Through meticulous study and comparison of the Bible, the Quran, and Jewish, Christian, and Islamic traditions, the author unravels the narrative of Abraham's commanded sacrifice. This pivotal episode, shared yet differently interpreted across these faiths, forms the core of the book. The author's investigation into whether Isaac or Ishmael was the intended son is both scholarly and accessible, offering readers a thorough understanding of the historical and theological context.

The book stands out for its balanced and respectful approach. The author emphasizes that her goal is not to undermine anyone's faith but to seek clarity and truth. Her narrative is enriched by personal stories, especially her reaction to online posts that mischaracterize Abraham, Hagar, and Ishmael, and her heartfelt shock at the hostility she found.

One of the book's strengths is its ability to engage readers of all backgrounds. The author's detailed examination of Abraham's story encourages readers to consider the deep-rooted connections and differences among the Abrahamic faiths. Her writing is not just informative but also thought-provoking, inviting readers to reflect on their beliefs and the historical narratives they hold dear.

The discussion about the defamation against Abraham and his family, the misinterpretation of Ishmael's status, and the subsequent rejection of Muhammad as a prophet provides a fresh perspective on age-old controversies. The author's use of scripture and tradition to support her arguments is compelling and well-researched, making the book a valuable resource for anyone interested in interfaith dialogue.

AUTHOR'S NEXT BOOKS

1. Jesus never taught the Trinity, it was invented after he left
2. Our only way to heaven as described in both Bible and Quran
3. Islam-the terminator of all evils [Written in reply to Evangelist Franklin Graham's comment about Islam being a very evil and a very wicked religion]